Dedication

I am grateful to reflect on a wonderful life and to reflect on the amazing promises of eternal life set before me with my Saviour and my Lord Jesus Christ.

In this book I have been able to give testimony of some of the people and situations which have shaped and encouraged that life. People who have been there in those moments when I went through the valleys of life. Situations that have challenged and strengthen my Christian faith. One lady I did not give credit to in the book has been the woman who has stood with me, whether on the hilltops, or in the valleys is my wonderful wife, Shirley. I also want to mention my children David and Deirdre who have been such a source of inspiration to me. The fact that they walk with Jesus has been a blessing which words cannot describe.

Contents

Foreword

P at and I have known Donald and Shirley for over twenty years, and they have been a great blessing in our lives. We have shared ministry with them and often enjoyed fellowship with them. We have always been blessed by their kindness and hospitality. They are Christian servants who believe, declare, teach and practice the four-fold Gospel - Jesus: Saviour, Healer, Baptiser and Coming King. The stories in this book are woven around this Gospel message.

Donald and Shirley are evangelists; they are pioneers; they are faith builders; they are missionaries; they are good Samaritans, who are following and living out the Gospel of the Lord Jesus Christ. Their ministry Centre is a place of warmth, welcome and wonderful food, where people feel loved and accepted and the Holy Spirit is at work, mending broken lives.

They are people who "tell it as it is." Donald is a great storyteller, and the stories in this book are true and told without exaggeration and without any hype or self-promotion. The incidents described actually took place as Donald has reported.

A Bible verse comes to mind: "And they went forth, and preached everywhere, the Lord working with them, and confirming the Word with signs following. Amen." (Mark 16:20). They have travelled the roads of Ireland, Scotland and Europe with the Gospel and God has confirmed their witness with signs of His presence. They have seen miracles, deliverances and healings such as Jesus experienced in Capernaum, Jerusalem, Jericho and the Gadarenes. Jesus said, "...he who believes on Me, the works that I do shall he do also." (John 14:12).

Donald and Shirley are following and believing the Words of Jesus.

They have also brought life-changing, practical help to many wherever they have gone. Their ministry has involved sacrifice and selflessness on their part, but what joy it has brought not only here on earth, but also in Heaven.

As you read this book, you will be inspired and encouraged. Donald writes "The main reason I wrote this book was to encourage people to seek God with all their hearts and the Scriptures say that they that fear the Lord shall do exploits."

As you read the stories, determine in your heart that you are going to seek God and, make this commitment, that you will obey whatever He calls you to do.

Let your motto be, *"BUT GOD ..."*

Marcus and Pat Thomas
November 2023

Pastor Marcus Thomas, and his wife Pat, now live in South Wales, where he was born. Although retired, Marcus is still active in Christian ministry. He is involved in sports chaplaincy, preaching regularly and writing Christian books. They had lived in Northern Ireland for over twenty years where Marcus had pastored churches, with Pat supporting him, as well as having her own fruitful ministry.

Introduction

I was born on the small Hebridean island of Benbecula in 1953. I was the youngest of four children, and my parents, John and Sarah, were hard-working and caring, and we lacked for nothing. My father worked for the Air Ministry as an engineer in a small power station at the airport. As well as holding down a full-time job, he also worked on a small farm (commonly known as a croft) in the Highlands and Islands of Scotland. He had about five or six cattle and some sheep on the croft. He also planted potatoes, wheat and hay, providing us with a fairly comfortable lifestyle (without us realising how blessed we were). He would also cut peat (turf) and sell a couple of trailer loads to help pay for the extras.

Like many others, my mother did not work until the children had all grown up. Then, she gained employment at the Ministry of Defence, on the military base in Benbecula. The language on the island was Scottish Gaidhlig (Gaelic), and English was seldom heard or spoken. I was eight years old before I began to learn English in the local junior/secondary school. I consider it a privilege to be one of very few people in the United Kingdom (or indeed in the world) who can still speak this beautiful language fluently.

Benbecula is a small island with an area of approximately thirty-five square miles. It measured about seven miles by five. My recollection of my childhood is a happy and carefree one. There was no electricity until I was about five years old, and I remember the tilly lamp hanging on the wall. Neither was there running water, and the entertainment was provided by neighbours and friends visiting and telling stories and "yarns." My favourite stories were ghost stories, which would "frighten the living daylights" out of me! I would then be afraid of going to bed and even more afraid to sleep. The visitors' stories were not always true, but they were very interesting and entertaining.

I looked forward to Saturday mornings, as on those mornings, one of my cousins came to visit and give a report of the events which occurred at the dance the previous night. It wasn't about the dance, but the fighting that went on outside the hall, the black eyes someone got, and the left hook another got! The fights could become clan against clan (the Morrisons against the MacRurys, for example), and others fought as one family against another. Sometimes, this cousin and his brother got involved in the fights, and generally, the fights were about nothing more than calling one another stupid clannish names. Although the fight was bare knuckle, everyone tried to come under Queensberry rules. There was to be no kicking or head-butting if possible. Weapons like knives or chains, etc., were totally forbidden.

GOD-FEARING RELIGION

On a religious front, there was seldom an issue. Our family was Catholic, and I did not know this until I went to school (as the Catholics and Protestants were separated and went to different rooms to have Religious Education), where we learned the Catholic Catechism. The Catechism was a booklet with questions and answers which you were encouraged to learn. Questions were asked, such as: who made you? To which the answer was: God made you. Why did God make you? And the answer was: God made me to know Him, love Him, serve Him, and be with Him in Heaven. You learned all these questions and answers in "parrot" fashion.

Going to church on a Sunday morning was almost compulsory. Cream buns for breakfast were an enticement and encouragement to get up and get ready. All your Catholic friends from school were there, and the children sat at the front, watched over by their schoolteacher. Any whispering or mischief in the pews was rewarded with a slap on the ear from the teacher. No parent ever argued or disagreed with this measure of punishment. Should they see it happen, the teacher was never questioned. Instead, you were given a good telling-off for your behaviour. "Shaming the family" was a phrase I sometimes heard. My parents were not into corporal punishment, but a mother's threat of, "I will have to tell your father when he gets home," was enough to quieten the mildest of uprisings, revolts, or rebellions.

At the age of ten, I was trained to be an altar boy. This was a job where you served the priest during the church meeting and brought the bread and the wine from a side table to the altar. A certain prayer the priest said was *supposed to* miraculously turn that bread and wine into the body and the blood of Jesus Christ. You were also in charge of ringing a bell at certain times during this religious ceremony called Mass. Being an altar boy was an ambition of every young Catholic boy at the time, and it was also seen as a sign of maturity (a "coming of age") to a certain extent, or the "Bar Mitzvah" of the Catholic Church. Ringing the bell at the wrong time was seen as a crime that was considered hell-deserving. For some families, it was the introduction for their boy to pursue the priesthood, but my family had no such delusions. You had to wear a white tunic with a belt around the waist, and you looked a little like a small monk. Later, I became a mercenary altar boy, only serving at funerals and weddings, where I got paid the princely sum of ten shillings (fifty pence) for the service provided.

THINKING OUTSIDE THE BOX

As I grew older, I began to question some of the teachings and ordinances of the Catholic Church. I remember asking God to make this real for me. I was never in doubt that there was a God, but my opinion of Him was that, to a certain extent, He was hard to please. I do remember that I feared God. As I went to confession, it was never in a state of repentance but to tick a box which kept my parents happy. At certain times during the year, you were encouraged to go to confession by your teacher or your parents. Easter and Christmas were important times on the church calendar. As such, confession was a compulsory act, if you called yourself a practising Catholic.

Although confession was something that you went to the local church to do, there were times when you went to Kileravagh School (a small school), where the priest would come and listen to you, as you went through the confession of your sins. I was quite proud of some of my sins and, at times, added a few extra to shock the priest! You confessed that you had sinned and were sorry for your sin. You could pretend you were sorry, as later on you would confess that you told lies, so an extra one would not really matter. You told him how many weeks, months, or years you were last at confession and then rattled out your list of sins.

As a child, I believed that he had the power to forgive sins. The priest would sit on a chair, and you had to kneel next to him, telling him the innermost secrets of your life. One day, I was speaking to an older boy about confession. I was about nine years old at the time. He told me that he had managed to simplify the whole process by telling the priest that he had broken the sixth and the ninth commandments, told lies, and that covered every sin in the book.

During my next confession time, I duly took my friend's advice and did it his way. The sixth commandment is: "You shall not commit adultery", and the ninth: "You shall not covet your neighbour's wife". Although I had no idea what the sixth and ninth commandments were at that time, I reckon the priest must have thought I was some sort of sex maniac, but he never questioned the matter!

Looking back on my upbringing in the Catholic Church, I believe that my questioning mind shaped me so as not to accept things at face value. I would still to this day consider myself a conspiracy theorist! Some of the loveliest people I have ever met have been Catholics, and I have great respect for their sincerity and conviction. Many have a very strong faith in their beliefs. Those beliefs are built equally on the Holy Scriptures and the doctrines and traditions of the Church. As a result of this, Catholics believe that they can pray to God through the intercessory power of the Virgin Mary and the saints. They sometimes use statues to remind them of a certain saint, or the mother of Jesus, in order to help them pray better. It is not the truth to say that Catholics pray to statues or see them as idols.

In the Holy Scriptures, it is written in John's Gospel (in chapter 14 verse 6): *"Jesus says to him, I am the way, the truth and the life: no man comes to the Father, but through Me."*

Another Scripture says in 1st Timothy chapter 2 verse 5: *"For there is one God, and one mediator between God and men, the Man Christ Jesus."*

In my understanding of truth, it was not necessary nor a requirement to have statues, rosaries and memorabilia to help us to pray, as the Scriptures in Romans chapter 8 and verse 26 tell us that the Holy Spirit will help us. The Bible verse reads like this: *"Likewise the Spirit also helps our infirmities: for we know not what we should pray for as we ought, but the Spirit Himself makes intercession for us with groanings which cannot be uttered."*

Many people were very critical of the decision I made to leave the Church, but I had no desire to be a hypocrite. I could not pretend to be someone I was not, nor could I go through the motions as if I was fully committed to them. I had gone through years of trying to understand what life was all about, and looking for someone who could help me and teach me the purpose of life.

There is one thing I remember with such clarity from those days. I could take you to the very seat where I was sitting (at St Mary's

Roman Catholic church in Griminish, Benbecula) when, in my heart, I cried out to God, asking for Christianity to be made real to me. It was a plea, a silent cry, saying: "Please, God, make this real for me. Make Yourself real to me. Make Yourself known to me."

OFF TO WORK WE GO

After leaving school, I went to work with the Royal Bank of Scotland, in a village called Lochboisdale, in South Uist. I did enjoy the work, and within a few years, I oversaw the travelling bank services (going around the villages with all the bank services provided from a Hillman Hunter Estate car). Banking, and life in general, were easier in those days.

In my early twenties, I was transferred to a village on the North-West coast of Scotland called Lochinver. Lochinver was a thriving fishing village, and the centre of all social activities was the pub in the Culag Hotel. While I was stationed in Lochinver, a crowd of us took a weekend out and travelled to Edinburgh, where I met a young lady called Shirley Graham. Shirley was from Northern Ireland and worked at the *Two Inns* restaurant in Frederick Street, Edinburgh. I had organised the event, gathering together almost fifty young men and women we had met in Lochinver during the summer of 1976. It was a form of reunion of old friends. Everyone I invited turned up for this occasion, apart from one young man, who phoned the restaurant to apologise for not being able to attend, as he was stuck on the Isle of Mull due to bad weather.

The restaurant also had a lounge bar, and we congregated there unannounced and caused some chaos to the manager and staff. They were short-staffed for the occasion, and Shirley was "run off her feet." To make matters worse, I gave her a bit of cheek and a hard time. She took an instant dislike to me, and it took me a long time to win her over, but I think that after forty-five years of marriage, I have finally managed it!

About a year later, Shirley came to live in Lochinver, having been invited there by a friend called Libby. This friend had managed to find employment for her in the Culag Hotel. It was here that the winning and the wooing began, and she will tell you that the only reason she went out with me was that in the winter months, I was the only person there who was available! Later on, I left the bank and went back to the islands to work with my brother, who had bought a grocery and hardware business and a petrol filling station. A short time after this, Shirley came to live in Benbecula and worked with us as a shop assistant.

MARRIED WITH CHILDREN

When I was twenty-five years old, I married Shirley in 1978, and we started off our married life living in a caravan at my father's house. Later, we moved to a small thatched cottage in a village called Balivanich. The cottage had been vacant for some time and needed some tender, loving care. By this time, our daughter Deirdre was born.

The cottage had a ghost story as part of its history. Although I had heard many ghost stories in my younger days, I no longer believed in a spiritual realm of ghosts or any paranormal stuff, but I was to be quickly educated. Some weeks after moving to this house, I got home from work one evening and found Shirley agitated and fearful. She was sitting with our daughter on her knee, telling me she did not like the house. "It has a strange feeling about it," she said. I convinced her it was just simply needing a wee coat of paint, and all would be "hunky-dory."

A few weeks later, I came home, and again, Shirley was quite concerned. "There is a strange feeling in this house," were her words, "and whatever it is, it is evil," she said. Once again, I was able to suppress her concerns. However, one night, a short time later, I came to a full understanding of her concerns. Through the night, I felt ill and needed to be physically sick. Whilst being sick in the bathroom, this strange presence enveloped me like a duvet wrapped around me, holding me but not hurting me. Scared and in fear, I went back to bed, not telling Shirley of my encounter with the evil she had spoken about. I was shivering, and when she asked what the problem was, I told her I was very cold (but I was being economical with the truth).

Although Shirley was raised as a Protestant, she agreed we should get the local priest in to bless the house. I went to see him and explained the situation. He came with "holy water" at hand and went into every room (throwing so much water that I thought he was trying to drown any evil spirits in the property)! The priest was Father Callum MacLellan, and I was unsure if he believed me,

10

although I believe he understood my concern for Shirley, who was so unsettled. We were on the council waiting list for a house, and he, being the local councillor, must have "pulled a few strings." Within days we were allocated a council house (where we stayed for twenty-two years). However, that night's encounter made me believe in a spiritual realm and was added to my understanding of life: that there was good and evil in the physical and the spiritual.

GOING INTO BUSINESS

My brother's business was doing well, and although I had a small investment (an estate car) in the business as a partner, it was decided that the business should be split after a few years. My brother and I worked together, but I took ownership of the mobile shop side of the business, and my brother kept the shop and filling station. We were both in agreement that this was the way forward. A bank account was opened in the name of: "The firm of D & S Buchanan." I believe that some sort of foolish pride came upon me at that time.

I saw myself as a bit of a "Del Boy" character in the islands. I did not limit myself to selling groceries, but anything and everything that would make a couple of pounds profit. I would buy second-hand cookers, fridges and freezers, fix them, and sell them on. I would sell beef fattening nuts for cattle and poultry grain for hens (as well as the groceries). We tried to be keenly competitive with our prices, but sometimes I had no profit margin on many of the goods we sold.

This business did make money (or so the tax man told me), but our spending was more than our income, which would eventually lead to disaster. By the age of thirty, I was deep in debt, owing the bank just under ten thousand pounds and other creditors another ten thousand pounds: a total debt of twenty thousand pounds. If you have ever been in debt, it is a trap that does not let you sleep at night, putting you in denial of the facts. The facts were serious, and the denial was even more serious. This situation brought tension into our home and, at times, into our marriage.

Although the debt was in the region of twenty thousand pounds in 1983, the figure would be over eighty thousand pounds in today's figures (the Office of National Statistics states that one pound in 1983 would have the buying power of four pounds in 2023). If you take the interest rate that the bank charged at that time, the debt was overwhelming. It was an impossible situation for any couple. *"But God..."*

SALVATION HAS COME TO THIS HOUSE

It was February of 1983, and I was still running the mobile shop to ensure that a lodgement was made to the bank to stop them realising the seriousness of my financial situation. I was still turning over about sixteen hundred pounds a week (which in today's money would be almost seven thousand pounds). In February of 1983, after a long day at work, I went home to find Shirley crying at the kitchen sink. I often say that it is hard to understand women, as sometimes they cry with happiness, and at other times they cry with sadness. In asking what was happening, she cried out: "Donald, I have been saved, I've been saved!" Not understanding the terminology, I inquired what that meant, as it was not in my vocabulary (apart from the football term where the goalie saved a shot at goals). She told me that she had gone to the MMG café (Mission to Military Garrisons), where they explained things to her about God and Jesus, and when she returned home, she repented of her sin and asked Jesus into her heart. She was *saved,* she said, *saved,* but I still did not comprehend this religious jargon.

Over the next few months, as tensions developed over Shirley's newfound faith and over money, I found her to have a certain calmness in the midst of the storms of our lives. Today, I would describe it as a peace that passes all understanding. She would read the Bible and be up in our bedroom praying. This stuff was doing my head in, as I had a fear of the Bible, originating from a story my mother told me many years previously.

At the age of sixteen, I had stayed at the Royal Hotel in Stornoway, where a Gideon's Bible was strategically placed by my bedside. It was the first time I had set eyes on a Bible. I had heard of such a book but had never seen one (never mind read one). It said at the front of this Bible, "Please do not remove this Bible, as the next guest may need it." This was almost an enticement for me to take it, and take it I did! On arriving home on Benbecula, my mother wanted my washing from my suitcase and found the Bible. She asked what this was, and I excitedly told her it was a Bible. I

13

had never seen a Bible before, and I was excited that such a book was in my possession, even though I had stolen it. She began to explain to me how dangerous this book was. "People have to study at colleges and Catholic Institutions to understand it," she said. It was dangerous because it could drive you insane, and she was quick to point out two people in the community who, at times, went insane and would shout in church during mass. So here I was years later with my wife, reading this dangerous book.

There were times when I believed that this book was following me. Although I exaggerate when I say that, it seemed that wherever I went, the only Bible in the house was there. If I opened the fridge, it was there, or the oven, or any cupboard in the house. This Bible seemed to follow me. Not only that, but my wife was reading it, and she would go crazy (no further comments allowed!)

Shirley's newfound faith intrigued me. I watched my dear wife to check for craziness, but only found love, joy and peace, and secretly wanted whatever she had. If it had been in a bottle, I would have drunk it. She never attacked my Catholic religion but would make small comments (usually late at night in bed) such as: "Do you call the priest Father?" "Yes," was my reply. Then she would tell me that the Bible instructs us not to call any man Father. This would rile me, but my beloved would turn over and go to sleep while I would be left fuming that I was unable to respond and at least get an argument out of it!

As the pressures of the debt increased, Shirley would say, "Put your trust in the Lord Jesus Christ, Donald." My immediate reply would be to ask her if He would send a cheque for twenty thousand pounds (for that is what we needed). To bring some constructive arguments to my corner, I borrowed a Catholic Bible from a friend, but what was in Shirley's Bible was very similar to the Catholic Bible. John 3:3, which was a big stumbling block, still said, "Except a man be born again he cannot see the kingdom of God." I knew I was not born again. I also knew I wanted to go to Heaven.

It was late on in 1983. I was under extreme pressure and saw no way out of my dilemma. I know of men and women who had taken their own lives when in such a predicament. Although suicide was never on the agenda, losing the children and possible imprisonment were things that I envisaged. There were no debt advisors in our small community. Debt was simply unacceptable and a real sign of a person's failure. There was no way out as far as I could see, but going on was becoming impossible. Shirley's advice to "Give it over to Jesus" seemed of little comfort, but I was in a situation where "Give it over to Jesus" became more inviting and enticing day by day.

SURRENDERING TO JESUS

Eventually, in December 1983, a humbled, broken man bowed his head and prayed a simple prayer in sincerity and in desperation. It said something like this: *"Dear Lord Jesus, I am a sinner, and I believe You died for sinners, so I believe You died for me. I ask you to forgive me for my sin. Come into my life Lord Jesus, and help me."* There were no conditions, but I simply wanted the peace that Shirley had, as I was "at the end of my tether." As I previously said, I do not recall having suicidal thoughts, but I can understand the pressure that has caused so many to get away from the awful mental pain debt can bring.

Nothing major happened that night. There were no flashing lights, no mist or fog came into the room, but Shirley told a Christian friend that I had surrendered my life to Jesus, and word soon went round the village. This word was not always popular, and I wondered if the craziness that my mother spoke about when she found the Bible in my bag many years previously, applied to me, as I was now reading the Bible to find comfort. It intrigued me, as I sensed a strength coming from the situations I read about. God taking over and setting people free from impossible situations was a source of inspiration to me at that time.

FACING THE OLD ENEMY

S oon, I found the courage to phone my suppliers (who were all creditors), explaining my situation and making a promise to work until every penny was paid. I was sincere with that promise but wondered how it would all pan out. I had such confidence that it would all turn out for the good, but I did not understand where the faith to have that confidence came from. Later, I realised that this faith was God-sent and that He was going to help me by taking me out of this pit of despair. Day by day, I began to turn to God in prayer, read the Bible and trust that God was for me. I had this total assurance that He would help me.

I began to work with my brothers, who knew nothing of the situation or my dilemma. They had both become successful in business; together, they had lorries, tractors, buses and diggers. My brother Allan also owned the shop and petrol station, as well as a Caravan Park. My other brother, John Alick, had a very successful garage where he sold cars and repaired vehicles that had mechanical problems or had been in an accident. He also had a petrol station. Business was prospering for both of them. They knew nothing about my debt and my embarrassment or the situation on a spiritual level.

Although I worked hard and diligently, the time came when word of my leaving the Catholic Church reached their ears. They were of the understanding that I had joined a new religion and forsaken my Catholic upbringing. Some people thought I had become a Buddhist, and others said I had joined the Bahá'i faith. The phrase "born again" was not well known on the island, and that was the phrase we preferred (rather than saying we were Christians or we had "come to faith"). The Gaidhlig word is *cùram (koo-rum),* and was used in Gaidhlig-speaking Christian circles. It speaks of being careful.

We felt that saying we were Christians did not fully describe our encounter with God. Within the family, there were some misunderstandings, and things were said and done that were regrettable on both sides. Sadly, the reactions to the situations took many years to be resolved and healed. It took me some time to understand that I had hurt both brothers (and my sister, who lives in Edinburgh). My deepest regret was that I had also hurt my father and mother, who were both retired and have since passed away. I now understand that it was their love and care for me which made them respond in the manner they did.

In those hard times, I was comforted by the encouragement of other believers, and I recall a very special home where we went to have fellowship. It was the home of Donald Ewen and Effie MacQuien from Tigharry. These meetings were often visited by people who had an experience of the revival in the Isle of Lewis (1949-53) and other encounters with God.

The home was always (and still is) welcoming to pilgrims. There was often a lot of singing (which I enjoyed), and there was always someone ready to share testimony. In those meetings, as a young Christian, I would sense the presence of God. I would come home comforted and encouraged to continue through the various struggles which life threw at Shirley and me.

At this time, life was extremely difficult, and we are thankful for those who came alongside us to encourage us. I realised that the cry I made in the Catholic church many years previously ("God, make this real for me") had now been answered. As I read the Bible, I realised the importance of the person called Jesus Christ. He became my hope in my difficult situation, my only hope for eternal salvation. I was now beginning to experience the peace that Shirley had demonstrated in her walk with her Saviour and Lord.

My brothers, in their attempts to bring me back to my senses (as they saw it), could no longer have a man working with them who was "shaming the family." In those dark days, I was drowning in debt, and with the interest rate at the time close to ten per cent, I was going deeper into debt every day. Within days, I got work on a construction site. My next employment was with a company called Rimmon Construction, which was building a school on the island. It was a testing time to join a squad on a building site who had all heard that I had gone "daft with religion." God gave me grace and patience, and after a short time, I won the respect of many of the men on the building site, with some even asking me about Jesus and my hope in Him.

GOD'S GRACE

Shirley had a part-time job in a local shop, which "kept the wolf from the door", but the wolf was getting closer to the door by the day. The wages on the building site only covered the interest at best, and now the bank manager phoned me, requesting that I attend a meeting with him in his office to explain the circumstances regarding my account.

As I entered the bank manager's office and took my seat, I realised there was a power within me. It was a power of simply trusting the Lord in a difficult situation. It was a trust that comes when all hope in self is lost, and everything is now entirely in the hands of Jesus. As the bank manager began to make demands for security and demanded that I sell my house to meet the debt, I was able to calmly assure him that my house was rented from the local authorities and that they would show extreme displeasure in my trying to sell it! He was not amused by my sense of humour! The van I drove was from the building site, and I had nothing to offer in my defence or to alleviate his concern. As his complexion changed, I found that he was in more trouble than I was. He was answerable to a Head Office, and I was answerable to God. And the God I now knew was going to be more understanding and gracious than his Head Office.

I made him the same promise as I did to the other businesses to whom I owed money. I was not considering bankruptcy, although it would have been easier for me, I knew deep within my being that everything was going to be alright, and nothing could sway me from that assurance despite the enormity of the task ahead. It was "a God thing."

A MAN OF LETTERS

During this time, letters in all shades, shapes and sizes were coming through our letter box. Many were from suppliers to whom we owed money, and a couple were letters from lawyers and solicitors threatening court action against us for the debt we owed. During this period, we had to choose who to pay and how much we could pay. We were renting the house from the local authorities, and (as we saw it) there was no pressure coming from them. Soon, the rent arrears we owed them accumulated. The local rent collector was very sympathetic, but it was now out of his hands, and letters were coming from the legal section of the Western Isles Council.

One day, two letters came, which were the same shade, shape, and size. One was addressed to Shirley, and the other was addressed to me. I opened mine and realised it was an eviction order from the Sheriff Officers. I quickly told Shirley not to open her letter, but she knew it was bad, really bad. Of all the moments of this period of our lives, I believe that this was the worst. But as we look back on it all, we somehow managed to get out of another horrendous situation by the grace of God. *"But God..."*

FAVOUR FROM GOD

Shirley and I had a small assurance policy with a company called Pearl Assurance. It was coming near maturity, and we expected over one thousand pounds, which would alleviate our desperate financial situation for a short time. The insurance man was Alasdair MacLean (Alasdair Ailean), and the night he called, he told me of a position coming up with the company. He encouraged me to apply for the vacancy but being unsure, I began to pray about it.

My prayer was answered the following Sunday when a man called Cecil Collins from Belfast was preaching in a small Christian Fellowship, which we attended as a family. This Fellowship had initially started in our home some time before, but now we met in a local school. The preacher knew nothing about my situation or of my considering applying for work with Pearl Assurance. He began preaching and told us that his sermon this Sunday morning was in two parts. He was first going to explain about "The *Pearl* of Great Price" (Matt 13:44-46) and then he was going to speak on our blessed *assurance* in Christ. He said, "My message is Pearl Assurance," and I nearly fell off my seat! God had spoken clearly into my heart.

I applied for the job with Pearl Assurance and got the position as an agent for the company. It involved collecting insurance premiums, selling car insurance, property insurance, pensions, life insurance policies and investments. Over the next ten years, I was one of the company's top salesmen, not only in Scotland but in the United Kingdom. Shirley and I were taken to the finals of snooker tournaments in Sheffield and Derby because Pearl Assurance sponsored the snooker, and sales records were being broken in this small catchment area in the Outer Hebrides. As sales increased, so did the wages, and every month the debt came down. As a result of interest rates and other charges the bank made, I do not know exactly how much we paid back, but eventually, after ten years, all the debt was paid in full. "*PAID IN FULL*," just as Jesus had paid for my sins on the Cross of Calvary. "*PAID IN FULL*." One company (which supplied fruit and vegetables in my days as a grocer) wrote to me and said I had restored their faith in human nature when I sent them the final cheque in settlement of my debt to them.

During that ten-year period, we both began to grow in the Lord. In those years, we encountered many obstacles and difficulties, but Jesus took us through every one of them. At that time, Benbecula had a military presence of one thousand soldiers and their wives. A number of the wives attended the Christian meetings, and, due to a lack of mature Christian men, I was appointed as "the Pastor." I knew very little of doctrines or theology, but we knew Jesus and His faithfulness. We began to see miracles, and signs and wonders, as promised in the Bible.

EXPERIENCING GOD'S POWER

One noticeable event happened in our hallway one day when a lady called Sylvia came in, almost crying with pain from arthritis and asking for prayer. We had people visiting us (as we often did). They were in the living room, so I decided to pray for her in the hall. I had never done anything like that before, but now, being "the Pastor," I believed that these were things which were expected of me.

My prayer was determined and sincere, to the point that my eyes were tightly shut. As I prayed, I heard a thud but refused to open my eyes, as I thought that it was the devil trying to disrupt me. Eventually, I finished praying, and there was no sign of Sylvia. I thought I had made her disappear or that Jesus had taken her! But then I found her on the floor almost behind me. The power of God had come over her and healed her, but there was so much power that it caused her to go weak at the knees and fall over. Since that day, I have seen many people overcome by this wonderful power, which is generally known in Pentecostal circles as "slain in the Spirit." It was a phenomenon that was experienced in the Ulster Revival of 1859 and many other moves of the Holy Spirit over the years.

At the time, I did not understand why this happened, but the power of the Almighty was too much to allow her to remain standing. Someone was asked, "Why do you fall over at times when someone prays for you?" They replied, "Because I simply could not stand." This was a new experience of God for me, and one I was to experience many other times in the future: of an Almighty God, doing almighty things.

Faith in God's Word was very, very real to us all in those early years and still is. You read it, you believed it and prayed for it to happen. In another part of this book, we will speak about the miracles and healings we have witnessed over the years, but the early days were simply exciting, amazing and faith-building.

On another occasion, there was a lady called Fay, who came to our meetings. Fay suffered from a problem with her back, causing a lot of pain and discomfort. We had heard that pain in the back could result from people's legs being different lengths. Sitting her comfortably on a chair, with her back tightly pushed back into it, we checked and found that there was a difference in the length of her legs. Calling several young people forward to experience the miracle of God which was about to happen, we prayed and watched (as if in slow motion), one leg growing to come into perfect alignment with the other. Fay's pain was gone, and she was marvellously healed.

THE BENBECULA FELLOWSHIP

The Fellowship was a source of inspiration to many over the years, and some of the local church leaders felt challenged by the amazing things that were being witnessed in the meetings. They further felt annoyed when some left their churches to become part of this Fellowship. Although we did not have a membership programme, many identified the Benbecula Christian Fellowship as their "church."

Some would stay as members of other churches but come to Fellowship with us and have fresh encounters with God's presence. Some other church members were warned to keep well away from us as we were perceived as a cult. Sadly, ministers tried to discredit us, but the more persecution we had, the more we were blessed. I was described as a hireling by one minister, and we were called names like "the happy clappies," and Shirley was called "the Hallelujah sister." These names were supposed to be detrimental to us, but we took them as badges of honour.

The Fellowship in Benbecula was being blessed. We introduced the only Scriptural example of baptism, by total immersion, which was mocked and ridiculed by many on the islands, but it was such a blessing to us. Culla Bay, Benbecula, where the full power of the Atlantic waves came crashing onto the shores, was our favourite place to baptise those who professed faith in the finished work of Jesus Christ.

One evening, an Army Officer's wife called Carol D (name withheld) attended the meeting in the house (which was packed, and the singing and praise were wonderful). In the middle of the singing, Carol raised her hands to Heaven and shouted in desperation, "I need to be saved. I want to be saved." Carol was led to the Lord in a simple prayer of repentance and salvation. This is an example of some of the experiences we enjoyed in those simple house meetings, as we gathered to worship the Lord and to share the Scriptures. There were no struggles to get people saved. God's presence was in the meetings, and things happened.

SANCTIFIED

Around this time, we had a visitor who was to become a great friend. His name was George Mackenzie, and later, we would meet his lovely wife, Mary, and family. We made many visits to Canada over the years. We even had a serious invitation from a church in Canada to become their pastor. George was brought up near Lairg in the Scottish Highlands. He was now ministering as a pastor in Alberta, Canada. He was a preacher and ran a church in Blackfalds near Red Deer (halfway between Calgary and Edmonton). George was different and very full of life and joy. He also wept easily when he sensed the presence of the Holy Spirit. One day, we had gone to an afternoon meeting and left George alone in the house.

Upon our return, he had tears in his eyes and said, "The Holy Spirit has been speaking to me about you guys." Immediately, I felt this sense of conviction of unconfessed sin in my life, and I needed to leave the room to get away from everybody. Although I had been saved for some time, this awesome sense of conviction had come over me. I went to the bedroom and wept and wept until I was in pain through weeping. I confessed any unconfessed and hidden sin in my life. I sometimes try to analyse what was said and try understand what caused this reaction, but for me, it was another release into the freedom that is found in Christ. A brokenness that only brings us closer to God. Some have told me it was a moment of sanctification, and I will settle for that.

THE BAPTISM IN THE HOLY SPIRIT

About that time, a lady called Shirley-Ann had come to the islands as the wife of an RAF serviceman. She told us all that she was baptised in the Holy Spirit and spoke in tongues. All this was new to many of us. I, for one, objected to this teaching, as some man who called himself a pastor had said it came from one of two sources: either the devil or God. He concluded that it was certainly not from God. This made me very aware and fearful of the teachings of this young woman. As I was now the "pastor of the Fellowship" I was vocal in my objections, but found this lady's worship, prayer life and understanding of the Scriptures at a level I had not previously encountered.

Unknown to me, some women were holding prayer times during the day, and Shirley-Ann was the one they were all looking to for guidance. Some asked for prayer to receive this Baptism in the Holy Spirit and found themselves experiencing God's presence and power. They also received this gift of speaking in tongues. Prostrations, "slain in the Spirit" (as described in the books written about the Irish Revival of 1859 and other revivals), were now happening amongst God's people in Benbecula. This was the same power that touched Sylvia in our hallway some time previously.

I also found that some of the ladies had a real zeal for God (including Shirley, my wife). One day, Shirley told me that meetings were taking place without my consent (I thought I was the big chief) but she had to confess that several of the ladies (including herself) had been blessed with this experience of the Baptism in the Holy Spirit, and that she too spoke in tongues.

I phoned George in Canada regarding this situation. I told him that they pray for one another, have experienced falling backwards, and sometimes heat going through their bodies. Others had been trembling, and all were experiencing speaking in new tongues (or languages - see Acts 2:4). To my horror, he said that this is all good, that it was very good. I was shattered, as here was a good friend taking the side of the "enemy" in my battle against the teaching of the Baptism in the Holy Ghost.

The Baptism in the Holy Spirit has been a source of many debates over the years. Some churches believe that this happens at the moment of conversion, when a person repents of their sin and is born again. Others believe that it is a subsequent experience and that the evidence of the Baptism in the Holy Spirit is "speaking in tongues" (see Acts 2:4).

It was understood that when Jesus breathed on the disciples (in John 20:21) to receive the Holy Spirit, that the life of God entered into them, making the experience in the upper room (Acts 2) a subsequent one at a later time.

THE ANOINTING OF THE HOLY SPIRIT

During this time, when I would preach, some women would stop me and tell me there was no anointing on my preaching. We had to stop the meeting and pray until the anointing came, and then I was allowed to move on. I did not fully understand the anointing until some time later.

We had a dear brother called Callum MacAskill from the Isle of Skye who came to visit us. During a meeting in the local school, after we had praised and worshipped God, we asked Callum to sing for us. Callum sang an old chorus which was popular with the Faith Mission. One line of the song said, "The thorns, they were placed on His beautiful brow, to pardon a rebel like me." At this point, everyone in the meeting began to weep and cry. Some fell to their knees and were broken by the words of the chorus. When the meeting was over, I spoke to Callum. I told him his singing was amazing and wondered when he could come back. Callum was a builder and had two houses to close off before the winter set in. He promised to phone me when he had a weekend break.

Six weeks later, Callum phoned to say that he had free time and that he would come back. I was so excited. I tried to get everyone to come and hear Callum singing. I told them of this wonderful man with the beautiful song, and the amazing voice that made us all weep. A few extra people came on the night of the meeting, and after a time of praise and worship, I introduced Callum, just as I had done at the previous meeting. He sang the same song to the same tune, and as we waited for something to happen. But nothing happened.

That evening, I learned that unless there is an anointing on what you do in the work of the Kingdom of God, it will have little to no effect. That night, I learned the importance of the anointing. On the first occasion, the meeting was under an anointing because Jesus was the centre of our worship, but the second time, it was our desire to be entertained. Meetings centred on the ability of men will never encounter the presence of God.

Sometime later, I began to seek for more of the Holy Spirit and this power, this gift, which is clearly Scriptural. I can never thank the Lord enough for this experience of blessing and empowerment of being Baptised in the Holy Spirit and the gift of speaking in tongues, along with other gifts (see 1 Corinthians 12), which have empowered and established my Christian walk.

MANNA MULTIPLIES

The Fellowship was now growing in numbers, and we were hiring the local school for our Sunday morning meetings. On this certain Sunday morning, six young people gave their hearts to Jesus and we were in celebration mode. Our agreement with the school was that we would be out at one o'clock in the afternoon, and the janitor would lock up, but we were not finished being together and fellowshipping. That day, we had invited Carol Arlow (now Anderson) and her two sons to lunch after the meeting. We had a small chicken, a boil-in-the-bag ham joint, some carrots, peas, and potatoes. We had enough for three adults and four children. Shirley decided to invite people back to our house and then announced that some of the RAF wives could bring their husbands (who were not at the meeting), and we would have lunch together.

Shirley and other ladies began serving the lunch. Plate after plate was filled, and everyone was fed. Now, if you have ever fed young military personnel, you will find that they eat more than the average bear! When the meal was over, someone asked where all the food had come from (as twenty-six people had been fed a full meal). We were all aghast as we realised that no one had brought anything extra, but God had multiplied the food. We cannot remember if any food was left over, but we suspect there was. We discussed and inquired about this matter repeatedly, and our conclusion is still the same today. *"But God..."*

EASTER CONVENTIONS
AND CONVERSIONS

Every Easter, we began to arrange what some referred to as a conference or convention. It was when friends and friends of friends came by invitation to the island, where special meetings were planned. Places to sleep and food were provided free of charge, and the time together was awesome. People would get saved and healed over these amazing weekends of fellowship.

One event was on an Easter Sunday morning when we would have an Easter Sunday service and break bread (have communion) together. There would usually be over one hundred people at the meeting. At this time, we met in an under-fives school in Balivanich. The room was divided, with one half having linoleum and the other half having carpet on the floor. As the communion table was positioned on the carpeted area, there was a one-way system around the back, up to the Table, and then back to the seat. It was observed that when people came off the linoleum onto the carpet, that many began to weep and cry. We sensed an anointing coming upon them as they approached the Lord's Table. If our memory serves us well, there were three young men (there may have been four) ready to partake of communion when suddenly the Holy Spirit descended upon them, and the tears began to flow uncontrollably. Tears streamed down their faces and noses and into the communion cup (in those days, there was one cup for everyone).

Two or three of these men are now ministers, and the other was a Christian youth worker. They had experienced a wonderful touch from God which I am unable to describe with words. I also believe that in those moments at Benbecula Christian Fellowship, their destiny was sealed by the Holy Spirit. Powerful experiences were normal at these conventions, especially at communion time.

There was another year when a "Holy Hush" came over the meeting as we finished partaking at the Table. Godly fear gripped us all in what could be described as an awesome moment in the presence of a Holy God. Having led the meeting, I was at a loss as to how to proceed. While quietly praying to the Lord, asking what I should do next, a young girl called Marion (aged about thirteen), stood up and began to sing an old hymn called, "It is finished, the battle is over." As she continued, other people joined in, and soon, there were voices of victory and celebration, punctuated by weeping and crying, in the midst of exuberant joy. Soon, there was a rapture of great excitement and expectation as the Holy Spirit was moving powerfully, reviving, restoring, and renewing His people. These meetings were never planned by men, but orchestrated by the Holy Spirit. These weekend meetings were God-ordained.

One young lady studying in Aberdeen was told about the Benbecula convention, as some called it. She had other plans, telling her friends she was going to something bigger and better in London. As she went to London, the Lord spoke to her that her need would be met in Benbecula. She took a flight from London to Glasgow and then to Benbecula. Every night she went forward for prayer but never made it to the front. The Holy Spirit met her in power every night, and she was flat on her back or face down in the aisle, being ministered to by the Holy Spirit.

We would have amazing speakers and amazing men and women of God speaking at these Easter weekends. There were men like Donald Saunders from Baltrushal, who was a steadfast Presbyterian at heart but a Pentecostal in spirit. I remember him sharing one evening and he brought a deep presence of God to the lectern. The preacher (Bruce Shimwell from South Africa) found it hard to stand behind that lectern as a result of the strong manifold presence of the Lord, which Donald had brought through his testimony and prayer.

Three men, Calum MacAskill, Steve Taylor, and Donald Saunders, were travelling to the meeting one day, and were passing a cyclist on a single-track road. The cyclist, a young lady from Liverpool, was struggling against a strong Hebridean wind. Being gentlemen, they stopped just ahead of her and rolled down the window to offer any assistance. She asked, "Where are you going?" and they told her that they were going to a Christian meeting. Throwing her bicycle into the ditch, she trusted them, took the lift and came to the meeting. After the meeting, she sought counsel regarding eternal matters and surrendered her life to Jesus. We followed her journey with Jesus for several years and one day will meet her in Glory. We have many stories of people having encounters with God outwith the meetings during these special times. You could say that the presence of God rested on the whole village at that time.

THE IRISH COME TO TOWN

The Easter meetings were now becoming well-known in many places. A group of some thirty people from Northern Ireland decided they would come. The late Jimmy Winning was the co-ordinator, and Shirley's mother, Mina, was one of those travelling in a bus they had hired. Mina made sandwiches for everyone, and leaving early, with many not having breakfast, the sandwiches were all eaten before the bus reached Larne.

Phillip Emerson (who is the senior Pastor at Emmanuel Church in Lurgan) was one of those included in that long journey. Although the plans were all with good intentions, they did not realise the time it would take to drive a bus round the twists and turns near Loch Lomond and into the Highlands to get to the islands. Another ferry journey brought them within twenty miles of their destination. At that time, we were amid the "Troubles" in Northern Ireland, and people were wary of every Irish accent. In people's thinking, there was the possibility that anyone having such an accent could be a terrorist. Benbecula was home to several hundred army personnel, and security was a little lax compared to other military establishments, as it was on a small island.

Shortly after these visitors arrived, we realised they meant business. Jimmy took some of the men and headed into a certain area called Tuzo Close to do some street preaching and share testimonies. The strong Irish accent was heard over the speakers from the bus, and soon, a serious security alert was in action as they were in the area where all the army officers lived. I got a phone call from the Regimental Police (as I had been cited as a collaborator). I had to attend the military guard room to vouch for their sanity and let them know that these people were no danger to the community. All planned open-air meetings were reluctantly cancelled, as we enjoyed a good relationship with the military personnel and did not want to spoil that.

That year, we had a demonstration of deliverance ministry. Jimmy Winning was the main man at Annaghanoon Christian Ministries, where people went for healing. Jimmy and others operated in a Christian ministry mostly unknown in the Highlands of Scotland. In their teaching, it is believed that a person could be demonically influenced and that Christians have the power to set such people free in the name of Jesus. Many Christians do not adhere to this kind of ministry, but having seen its effects, you will be left in no doubt that God can set people free from many situations in the name of Jesus.

AUTHORITY IN THE NAME OF JESUS

At an evening meeting, Jimmy began to teach about his own specialist subject, demonology. We never harnessed preachers but gave them freedom with the subject of their choice. Although Shirley and I knew a little about the subject, we were shocked by Jimmy's choice. We would have preferred something safer and gentler. He explained his subject, quoting various Scriptures and giving testimony of various cases he had personally experienced. There were several pastors in the meeting that evening, and you could sense discomfort as Jimmy came to the end of his preaching and teaching. He then did an altar call (which means that people were invited to the front to be prayed for). A lady called Ellis was one of those who responded.

Explaining that she had suffered from backache for several years, she told Jimmy how incapacitated she was because of her condition. She said that she had tried every conceivable medical help she could find but to no avail. Jimmy (quietly spoken and gentle) told her it was possibly a demon, asking where the pain was in her back. She explained that it was at the base of her spine and that she felt pain going down her legs and, at other times, up the back of her head. "Oh!" he said, "that sounds to me like the spirit of Kundalini."

He further explained that this spirit is commonly associated with people who practice yoga and other Eastern exercises and religions. Ellis confessed that she had been involved in yoga exercises (not the chanting, but just the exercises). Jimmy went on to explain that it was like an octopus sitting at the base of her spine, and its tentacles could stretch to whatever part of the body it wished to affect. He told us that Christians had the authority in Jesus' name to command this spirit to leave, for its power to be broken off her, and that she would be set free. Shirley and I stood beside her when Jimmy spoke with authority: "In the name of Jesus Christ, I command you, spirit of Kundalini, to leave this body now," he prayed. Ellis screamed the most awful scream, which pierced the atmosphere. In the congregation, people rushed to the door to leave. Some pastors were seen throwing their children over chairs to get them out. There were scenes of devastation in the congregation, but the demon was cast out, and Ellis was healed. She was bending over, touching her toes, and exercising her newly found freedom from pain for the first time in many years. Whilst many in the congregation had scattered, the atmosphere in the building was not of Christians celebrating a sister set free but anger that such a thing should happen in a Christian meeting.

Later that evening, the upset it caused was being expressed very vocally and verbally. It was directed at Shirley and me, as we had made the arrangements for these meetings. My reply was for those objecting to speak to the lady, ask her if she was healed, and understand her joy of being healed through the expelling of a demonic entity. Slowly, the heat was taken from their fire as Ellis explained what had happened to her and the freedom and joy she experienced. There could be no doubt that this was God operating in a ministry many had not previously known anything about. It was necessary to consider the matter with a better understanding of the Scriptures, where Jesus commanded demonic deliverance and people were set free.

The following morning, there were still a few irate people around, and the speaker was a young man called Scott Cameron. In his own gentle way, he spoke of the Christ he loved and adored. Through a wonderful, gentle spirit that rested on him, everyone was pacified. You felt that God had anointed Scott to be a peacemaker. Scott has been the minister at Stevenson High Kirk for many years. Stevenson was also the hometown of the late Jimmy Winning.

DELIVERANCE

As we went on, Shirley and I became more involved in this ministry of deliverance, helping many people. Some came specially from mainland Scotland to Benbecula for help. One evening, we had a meeting in our own home, and a lady had crossed over on the ferry to come to us for prayer. Although she attended a well-known Pentecostal Church, she was embarrassed about her condition. We had many teenagers coming to our meeting at the time, and we ushered them out of the living room. We asked them to pray on the stairs and in the hall as we made preparations to minister to this woman in the living room of our home.

After a short time of prayer and ministry, the lady was set free. I went out to tell the young ones to come back in, but there was no sign of them. As I went to my daughter's bedroom, I knocked on the door, and she answered. I will never forget the look on her face. She was shining, she was glowing and blurted out: "Dad, Dad, the Holy Spirit has been here," and that her friend had been set free from a demon. This young girl was lying prostrate on the bed, under the anointing of the Holy Ghost (or 'slain in the Spirit"). The peace of God was all over her face, and God had ministered supernaturally through the ministry of these young people, who had previously never known anything like this.

It was a moment of great rejoicing but also a moment of great concern. The majority of those young people were going home to parents who knew nothing about the ways of God and could have questioned the activities taking place at those Holy Ghost meetings. Praise the Lord, no one ever did, and many parents actively encouraged their children to attend.

There were so many experiences in those early days in that small fellowship of believers, away in the west, in a small Hebridean island called Benbecula. We knew very little about theology or doctrinal matters, but the presence of God was very near and very real. The Holy Spirit was teaching us the theology and the doctrines as we went, and the knowledge was in our hearts, not our heads. Meetings were places of excitement and expectation.

The house would be packed with joyful voices singing praises to the Lord. There was expectation as to who would be saved, who would be healed, who would be set free. The name of Jesus was sweet on our lips. People would get healed, people got saved, and we influenced many military personnel who took the Gospel far and wide as they were posted out from Benbecula.

One man phoned me some years later. He told me that the night he came to our house, he was an atheist, and I had spoken about the sheep and the goats. He could not get it out of his thoughts that he was hellbound, and sometime later, he put his trust in the Lord. The day he phoned, he told me he was now preaching the Gospel, and he had, that same day, baptised the first person he had led to Jesus for salvation.

PLANS FOR OUTREACH

With a desire to share the Gospel, we considered buying an old-fashioned large TV system with three colours reflecting onto a mirror, which then made an image on a screen or wall. Some older people will still remember these televisions, which were often found in public houses. Things like overhead projectors were not yet invented. Our desire was to show Christian films, with plans to get into care homes and schools. This was during the lean years of debt, and although working through it, finances were still very strained. I phoned Rank Film Distributions, a huge organization, for advice regarding our plans. They used to lend equipment to show films, but now we were in the more modern world of VHS and Betamax video tapes.

This man told me of a Christian friend (from Poole, in Dorset) who was selling equipment to show videos. With the sale of the equipment were two hundred Betamax videos of Christian films and preaching, as he was changing over to VHS videos. Poole in Dorset and Benbecula in the Hebrides could not be much further apart in the UK! The man from the Rank Organisation asked me not to tell his friend what he had told us about the plans of the man in Poole, as he was not quite ready to sell. When I phoned the man in Poole, he told me that the asking price would be in the region of one thousand two hundred pounds. This figure was completely out of the question for me to buy, so I set it aside.

A week or so later, he phoned me to ask how I knew he was selling it, to which I replied that I was not at liberty to tell him. "Where do you live?" he asked. When I told him, he said, "Brother, this is God. Because I believe this is God, I will reduce my price to one thousand pounds." I requested time to pray for this situation. I phoned a few friends (there was no Facebook, etc., in those days!) to ask them to pray, and some replied with encouragement. However, one said this was not of God and to stay well clear. Another had a scripture from Habakkuk 2:3: "For the vision is yet for an appointed time....... wait for it; because it will surely come, it will not tarry.." I began to feel this was the Lord's leading,

42

although the negative voice was still ringing in my ears. I prayed, "Lord if this is from You, make me a way of escape."

Not having the money to buy it, I had to go and borrow the money from a different bank. The man would deliver it to Eyemouth, near the Scottish Border, in the east of Scotland. I would make the plans to collect it from there. I had a friend there called Hector, who had island connections and ran a Christian youth work. It was delivered to him, and he requested to use it one evening. It was a cumbersome big thing, weighing two hundredweight or more. It was at Hector's house for several days, and then he phoned me. "Donald," he said, "if for some reason you do not use this, I would be happy to buy it off you." That was my way of escape if things did not work out.

After I collected it and took it back, the system was set up in our living room one evening. We were going to show a video of Billy Graham preaching (there were no "God channels" in those days). Because the negative voice was still coming to my ears now and again, I asked the Lord that if this was His work, someone who was not saved, not born again, would come, and through this ministry would surrender their lives to Jesus. The request was clear and specific.

A DOUBLE PORTION

The first evening that we used this new equipment to show a video, the living room was full, but to my sorrow, everyone professed salvation. Everyone there believed they were Christians. Billy Graham preached, and I can still remember his sermon about faith and believing God's Word. I sat there dejected, as no one could fulfil my prayer request. But at the end of the video, a beautiful young RAF wife called Sharon said, "I am a Sunday school teacher and always thought I was a Christian, but tonight I realise I am not. I haven't got what you people have. I do not have what Billy Graham preached about. I want to be saved. I need to be saved." After repentance, prayer and acceptance of Christ as her Saviour and Lord, she became concerned about what her husband would say. I asked her to phone him, and should he be annoyed with her, we would send a couple of "heavies" home with her to sort him out!

She told him what had happened over the phone. He said that she had left her Bible behind, and he had been reading it. "Is there someone there who can explain some of it to me?" he asked. A short while later, he arrived, and after explaining the Scriptures to him, he was ready to accept Christ as his Saviour and Lord. His wife, who was newly converted herself, led him to Jesus with the help of others. It was a glorious moment. It was another *"But God..."* moment.

THE FRAGRANCE OF JESUS

Although we enjoyed fellowship together at the local school, the house meetings were the jewel in the crown. Holy Ghost experiences were never far away. Another evening, another meeting, we were enjoying each other's fellowship. We would sing and make a joyful noise unto the Lord. There was no worship leader, and often, there were no musical instruments, but we sang and sang again. We also enjoyed the sharing, the preaching and the teaching of the Word of God, as it was so fresh and refreshing to many of us.

The meeting was over, and after enjoying a cup of tea, Shirley-Ann (previously spoken of) asked what the lovely fragrance was. We were formed in a circle in the living room of our home, and then someone else said, "There it is." "Oh, it is so lovely," said another, "that fragrance is so beautiful." In a short space of time, this fragrance was circulating and wafting around the room. It was a bit like the old Bisto advert we used to see on the television when they sensed the smell of the gravy and said, "Ahhh...." Some people had to go home as it was now nearly midnight, and one lady called Effie (from Tigharry) said, "It is Psalm 133." Others who could stay did not want to leave or move.

One young RAF serviceman called Andy told me that the fragrance was on his hands, but all I could smell from his hands was nicotine (as Andy was a young Christian who had not yet been set free from smoking). Shirley and I went for a walk at four in the morning, and this beautiful fragrance enveloped us as we walked in a strong Hebridean wind. The next day, we phoned Effie to tell her of the continuation of the fragrance through the night hours. Her husband, Donald Ewen, was upstairs and called down, "Effie, what's the lovely fragrance in the house?" As crazy as it seems, this fragrance, which we believe was the Lord's presence, travelled through the telephone lines to a home twenty-plus miles away.

Later, a similar story came to our ears as Effie phoned a dear friend called Rita. As Rita was being told this remarkable story, her mother cried from the living room, "Rita, what is that lovely fragrance in the house?" Experiences such as this were reported during the Lewis Revival of 1949-53 but were never recorded. However, the late Reverend John Smith (the first man saved in the Lewis Revival) assured us that such an experience had been known at that time.

MIRACLES AT THE FIRESIDE

Helen was a friend and a neighbour. She was from a Free Church of Scotland background (Presbyterian) and not prone to an understanding of the supernatural or spiritual gifts. Helen was the local lady who, in the springtime, took all the orphaned lambs in the area to feed and care for them. She had been saved and was possibly trying to balance her church background with the new things she was being taught. Helen had hurt her hip and was in a lot of pain.

One night, she came over to our house for a wee visit, and as she stood in front of the fire, we were speaking about her injury. I quoted from Romans 8 and verse 11: "But if the Spirit of Him that raised up Jesus from the dead dwell in you, He that raised up Christ from the dead shall also quicken your mortal bodies by His Spirit that dwells in you." She said, "I believe that, you know. I really believe that." There was a sound like a loud crack. In asking what it was, Helen immediately spoke up and said, "I've been healed, I've been healed!" And she *was* healed, yes, completely healed. No one had prayed for her, laid hands on her, or anointed her with oil, and here she was, totally healed. She had simply believed God's Word and was marvellously healed. Hallelujah! *"But God..."*

GOD-GIVEN DIRECTIONS

Another situation happened when Sandi, a lovely young RAF serviceman's wife, walked into our living room one day. Sandi was a Christian girl who did not work (nor did she want to work) as they were in a secure financial position, and she loved being a wife and a mother. Immediately, I began to tell her that the Lord knew she was a good wife and a good mother, and wanted her to help other mothers who were struggling in their lives. It is apparently known as a "Word of wisdom". (1 Corinthians 12) Within days, Sandi got a phone call from Social Services, asking her if she would consider taking a job helping young mothers who were struggling. As a result of the Word she had received a few days earlier, she accepted the position. Soon, she was contacting several young mothers, helping and encouraging them, as well as teaching them the basics of motherhood and housekeeping.

One day, Sandi phoned us with a dilemma. She had been assigned to a young mother called Janette (name used with permission) and, upon calling with her, had found that there was a situation she was not able to cope with. A man who had lived in the home had been hurting them by his behaviour. He was now gone. We were invited to help in what was a difficult situation. As a priority, we felt that Janette needed to move to another house, as her home had too many wicked memories. Soon, Janette and her young daughter were in a new house less than one hundred yards from our home. Shortly afterwards, there was another man visiting her. We were watching out of concern and wondered what was wrong with this woman, having another man not only visiting but staying overnight at times.

We tried to give this young lady space, and knowing that she had a dislike (or should I say a distrust) of Christians, we felt it was right to do so. Within a period of time, we did meet the boyfriend. His name was Anthony, and there were plans for him to be a husband. Not too long after this, I was visited by the couple, asking me if I would marry them. I asked where, when, and why, but it was all a bit hazy, and I thought that it was better for them to be married than live together. With their permission, my wife Shirley and I made plans. There was an old shooting lodge in South Uist where they could get married in one of the staterooms. Bella and the other staff working there were helpful and excited at the possibility of having a wedding in Grogarry Lodge. They were willing to cook a meal for us, as they would have plenty of venison, salmon, grouse and other choice foods left over, after the hunting season had come to an end. Plans were made for the day and the hour.

On the special day, there were twenty guests invited. The best man was a drug user and possibly a drug pusher. Janette's mum was a lady who liked to organise things and looked very busy. Some of the guests I would know and find hard to like, but they were their friends, and I had to carry out a very important duty on their behalf.

As I proceeded with the ceremony and the wedding vows were being said, people began to weep and cry. Janette's young daughter was crying, the bride's mother was crying, and the best man was crying, as were many others. In desperation, I inquired of the Lord as to what was happening, but there was no reply. I continued the wedding ceremony, pronouncing them man and wife. I thought, "This is a mess. This will never last." Knowing the Holy Spirit was touching lives, I thought to pray for the married couple. As I stammered through a prayer, pretending all was well, we ended up having a lovely meal together. Then the young couple went back home with plans to go on honeymoon later.

The next day, Janette appeared at our home a little bemused, asking for Shirley. I immediately thought that there had been a big argument and the marriage was over. A wee while later, Anthony appeared and wanted to speak to me. "Look, mate," he said, "when you prayed for my wife and I yesterday, a powerful current of electricity went through my body; what was that?" I explained to the best of my ability that it was the Holy Spirit (little knowing that indoors, his new wife was explaining a similar experience to Shirley). They had not conferred with one another, fearing that one would think the other had a mental health issue.

A few evenings later, the couple came back. The wife wanted to speak to Shirley privately, and in the conversation that followed, she wanted to pray a sinner's prayer, to repent of her sin and ask Jesus into her heart. As she appeared at the living room door with a broad smile, she announced, "I have given my heart and life to Jesus," to which her husband cried and said, "What about me?" "Oh," she said, "I cannot save you, but maybe Donald will help you make your peace with God." Spending time explaining the doctrine of grace, this man also accepted Christ as his Saviour. (Please note: we did not know it was the doctrine of grace).

This couple is still together and still very much in love after all these years. We recently met up with Janette, and she and Anthony are really well. I let her read what I wrote about her, and all she wanted to add was that at that moment in time, she had lost all trust in people, and in humanity, but we were there to help her get her life back again.

THE MAN WHO STUCK TO THE FLOOR

Another peculiar situation happened when a man called Paul and his family came to the Fellowship meetings. Paul and Susan had two children, and Paul was strong-willed, opinionated, yet very likeable. We had no doubt they were real Christians, but life was a bit of a struggle for them. They lived in a caravan, and he did not work.

One day, during a discussion, we were saying that God was unlimited in His power. Paul disagreed. I said that if God wanted to stick him to the floor, God could. He rubbished that comment and said God couldn't do that.

Being all in agreement with the original statement, Paul got a bit annoyed and tried to ridicule the thought that God was all-powerful. Suddenly, he became stuck fast to the floor. He became agitated and angry, believing we had done something to make this happen, but he was unable to move. Although we found this so hard to believe, we pretended that we were in a place of total understanding of the situation, which we were not.

We advised him to repent of his comments but he refused. After a time, we got him a chair, as his legs were getting sore trying to remove his feet from the spot where he was stuck. His young girls went over and said, "Are you stuck, Daddy? That's very funny!" To which he had to reply in an angry voice that he was stuck. After a good period of time, he prayed and repented of his comments and was immediately released. There are some situations in life where you have to be there to believe it, and this was one such incident. *"But God..."*

Paul and Susan had never been married and were the first couple I married. When we first met them, we understood them to be a young couple with two children. One day, Paul asked me to marry them, which was such a shock to the system as I believed they were already married. So without much fuss, we arranged for a local hotel to provide us with a room and light refreshments. After the wedding, it was back to our house, where Shirley had cooked a small dinner.

KEVIN AND KIM'S WEDDING

Paul and Susan were the first two people I had ever married. It was a good wedding, but one that always brings a big smile to my face was the wedding of Kevin and Kim. Kim was a lovely young girl we had met years before, and she attended the Fellowship with her family. The marriage ceremony, however, was going to be in a hotel in Aberdeen, and I was offered the privilege to officiate. Kim made a beautiful entrance into the room where the marriage ceremony was to take place. She wore a wedding dress in a style which had rings or hoops to embellish its beauty. As Kim stood in front of me, this dress seemed outstanding in every sense of the word. I asked her if she could sit down, and she told me she could not, the reason being the hoops or the rings.

Not understanding the enormity of the situation, should she sit down, I asked her to sit, as she was standing directly in my way of seeing the people I needed to speak to and share about Jesus. As Kim sat down, a full explanation of her dilemma came to light and into sight. Sitting down caused the hoops in the dress to lift the dress over Kim's head! It caused the upper part of her body to disappear and the lower part of her body to be exposed (although she was able to keep a certain moderation of decorum). It was eventually agreed that Kim should stand a little to the side so I could see the other people.

Kevin and Kim have recently celebrated their twenty-fifth wedding anniversary, but their wedding day was a day to remember!

KARL AND CATHEY'S WEDDING

Another marriage I remember with fond memories was that of Karl Reece and Cathey Miller. They had met at a beach called Culla Bay, Benbecula, at the tender age of sixteen and were engaged shortly afterwards on that very same beach. It was an automatic choice that they would be married at that beach. I had a license (unlike many other ministers at the time) where I could marry people outside a church building. When I sent the request to the Registrar's Office in Edinburgh, I was told that officiating outside was always dangerous, as the weather may not be suitable for such a special occasion. She told me that should a gale-force wind be blowing, should the heavens open with thunder and lightning and should it pour with rain, the marriage ceremony still had to take place there, or it would not be legal. Agreeing with her and sharing her concerns, I spoke to Karl and Cathey. But Culla Bay, it had to be.

Beautiful Culla Bay, Benbecula
(Picture By Lena MacPherson, Benbecula)

It was the month of May in Benbecula, and a very cold wind blew in from the sea. The groom and the best man waited near a trellis that Marion, Karl's mother, had created and made into a work of art. The trellis was to give a focus on the main event. I came along wearing an old, heavy army coat to keep myself warm, and not having the proper understanding of the trellis' purpose, I hung this old coat on it. The bride arrived across the sands with her bridesmaids, all looking beautiful in their dresses. However, the bride's and the bridesmaids' dresses gave little or no protection from the stiff wind blowing in from the sea. The wind was also blowing the sand in our faces.

As I began the marriage ceremony, I looked at the bridal party; their lips were turning blue with the cold. My own daughter, Deirdre, was one of them, and the bride's sister, Sandra, another. To say it was "Baltic" is an understatement. I realised that if the bridesmaids were going to survive, I would have to hasten the proceedings. The wedding vows and promises were made in record time! The old coat catching the wind had taken its toll on the trellis, and it stood like the leaning tower of Pisa before the marriage ceremony was over. The old coat had, however, managed to be in every photograph of the wedding ceremony! Although the trellis did not survive the day, Karl and Cathey have survived twenty-five happy years of marriage.

GOD-SENT GIFTS

Over the years, God has sent us men and women who were gifts to us to encourage us and build the body of Christ.

I have mentioned many of these people, but I have also not made mention of others who came to a small Scottish island and were a great blessing (and I am sure they were blessed in return).

If your name has not been mentioned, please forgive me and get in touch, as in the next book, I will write a whole chapter about you.

SAMUEL McKIBBEN

One of the people who took a real interest in us when we were a fledgling young Fellowship in Benbecula was Samuel McKibben. Samuel was a pastor of the Apostolic Church in Inverness and was the man God used to plant Inverness Christian Fellowship. He made regular visits to Benbecula, and his preaching and teaching were alive and exciting. He encouraged us at that time, and one of his elders was another man from the Hebrides, a certain Ronnie MacLean. Ronnie was a recognised prophet in the Apostolic Church. We were blessed by both men as they ministered. We had a lot to learn, and those men gave of themselves to help us grow in the Lord. The people in the Inverness Christian Fellowship took us under their wing for a time, and we were strengthened by their friendship.

There is one particular meeting I remember, and it was a time when they invited us to join them in Inverness for a weekend of fellowship. We met at Culloden Academy, and after some praise and worship, the atmosphere changed, and the presence of God was as a mist over the meeting. Ann Coppard, a lady from the Inverness Fellowship, began to prophesy and spoke right into the lives of men and women, giving details of their lives as if she had known them for years.

In the prophetic utterances, there was direction for some and encouragement for others. My recollection was that as the Lord touched me, the Spirit of joy filled my soul, and I began to laugh and laugh in the joy of the Lord. Shirley was on her hands and knees on the floor, crying and sobbing, and I remember thinking how awful I was not to be comforting my dear wife. God was doing something different with each of us at that moment in time.

ELIZABETH AUSTIN

When we were in Benbecula, we had some amazing visitors over and above those who came to the Easter meetings. Elizabeth Austin had cancer in her jaw when she was younger and had promised God that she would go and be a missionary in Africa if Jesus healed her. Elizabeth was marvellously healed, and fulfilled her promise by going to Africa as a missionary. She was one of our favourite visitors. She was introduced to us by Tom and Jean Somerville from Northern Ireland. The only image I had of her, as I went to collect her at the small airport in Benbecula, was what Tom had told me: that she was an American woman who was a missionary in Africa.

My thought pattern visualised a greying elderly lady dressed in drab clothing, but the lady I met was very different indeed. She was a miniature Dolly Parton, with blonde hair and very red lipstick. She was wearing a red leather trouser suit, and my first impressions were negative, but that was soon to change. Elizabeth heard clearly from God.

Her first statement was that we had a man in our fellowship who would try to convince us that he was one of us but was still clothed in his own filthy robes of self-righteousness, never having adorned the garments of salvation or Jesus' robes of righteousness. We had a disquiet about a certain man who was coming to the meetings at that time, and he was impressing some of the younger Christians with his ability to quote the Scriptures. We were, however, very wary of him. She warned us of this person, and over the days we were with her, we entered into another realm of living at a higher supernatural level with her teachings and prophetic utterances, which were precise and accurate. They were to help and encourage us for the days ahead, giving us a vision for the future.

BRUCE SHIMWELL

Another man who influenced our Christian journey was Bruce Shimwell. This man from South Africa carried a wonderful anointing and had a teaching ministry. It was teaching which we drank like a beautiful wine (if we drank wine).

One night, he preached for three hours, and we did thirst for more. Bruce was a travelling preacher man. Once, he was in Alice Springs, Australia, when he was asked if he knew of a Benbecula Christian Fellowship. They said that the Lord had told them to pray for the people in that Fellowship, but they did not know where it was (these were days before we had Google!) To us, that was, and still is, amazing: that God can stir His people on the other side of the world to pray for some insignificant people in the Hebrides in Scotland

Many names I could mention could have testified of their input into our lives, and we remember many stories of their exploits in Benbecula.

THE WELLS OF SALVATION

Another couple who blessed us and intrigued us were Alfred and Eileen Wells. They appeared, it almost seemed, out of nowhere one Sunday morning as we were at our meeting in Balivanich School. As soon as they walked in through the door, we loved them, and they loved us. There was something about them which was warm and friendly. As we look back on those differing situations, we now know that they carried the presence of the Lord.

After the Second World War, it was difficult to get work. Alfred worked for a farmer, and Eileen was bringing up the children. They had eight boys and one girl, but I do not know how many they had at that particular time. One year, Alfred attended an exhibition with the farmer who employed him, which was something like an Ideal Home exhibition. There, businesses and individuals were showing off their products and inventions, especially regarding making life easier and more comfortable. Electrical goods and gas appliances were the main features, and Alfred overheard someone say, "Whoever makes a good solid fuel burning fire would do well for himself in the years ahead. All these new-fangled ideas will soon be outdated." Alfred and Eileen had been Christians from a young age and would teach and believe in praying about their plans.

This plan of making a solid fuel-burning stove was burning in his thoughts. There was welding equipment at the farm, and soon Alfred was spending every available moment in an old shed to bring his plan and idea to birth. One year later, he had a prototype of a solid fuel-burning stove and brought it to the exhibition. An elderly man came along and made inquiries regarding his invention. Alfred was happy to answer all his questions, and the man said this was exactly what he had been looking for. He asked if Alfred had a factory and what it was called. Alfred took liberty with the truth and told the man that the name of the factory was Charnwood, which was the name of the forest behind the farm.

To his joy and excitement, the man gave him an order for twenty stoves, and the business of AJ Wells and Sons was born. Over the years, the business had flourished and been blessed. Charnwood Fires are some of the most efficient and most popular of the fires and stoves for sale throughout the United Kingdom and Ireland.

I could tell many stories about Alfred and Eileen. They were a retired couple who loved nothing more than sharing times around the Word of God. You could ask Alfred to share a Word any time of the day or night, and he believed in a simple verse of Scripture: "Open your mouth wide and I will fill it" (Psalm 81:10). We had many wonderful nights around the Word of God, with Alfred and Eileen challenging, encouraging and blessing us.

One story I will share was of their faith in God to stand in difficult times. The business had grown, and now they had a factory in the Isle of Wight. Eighty people were employed by Charnwood Fires, and many homes were dependent on them for their livelihood. Five of the boys worked in the business, but Alfred was still in charge at this time. It had been a very mild winter, and the economy had gone through a difficult time. There was a recession in the country, and sales and profits came to a very crucial situation. Cash flow was not happening, and consideration was given to making many of the employees redundant. This would have been the normal procedure in a business, but Alfred believed that with prayer, things could turn around.

Many in the factory were Christian believers, but many were not. Gathering the employees together, he explained their position but told them they had built this business together and every person there was a part of its success. He made a promise that no one would be made redundant, but should there not be a turn around, the whole business would close down. He then turned to the Christians and asked them to come to a prayer meeting thirty minutes before work every morning. He also told those who did not profess Christianity that they would be very welcome to attend and call on God to provide their need. Every morning, the gathering crowd grew, and a large majority of the workforce came to pray or agreed with others in prayer.

It was getting near crunch time. The bank was making ugly noises, and every one of Alfred's family had re-mortgaged their homes to the hilt. There was no space left for them to play with, and sad thoughts of winding up the family business were forming in their minds.

One day, two official-looking men carrying briefcases came into the factory, asking to see the management. Everyone thought they were tax inspectors or some other government officials. Some thought they were from the bank and were there to close down the business. They met Alfred and some of his sons in the office to discuss a project. They were from the London Underground. They explained their mission was to replace all the signs in and around London's Underground system with new signage. They had been advised that the most lasting and permanent signs were enamel ones, and they had decided to use this type in the underground system. They had come to ask Charnwood Fires if they were in a position to consider this contract they were offering. Alfred explained the cash flow situation at the company, the expenses of altering the machinery and all the other problems that went with the work.

Those official-looking men explained to Alfred and the boys that expenses were not a problem, asking if it was possible, to which the answer was yes: it was possible. They went on to tell Alfred that his business had come with the highest recommendations of honesty and integrity. They continued to say that Charnwood fires had a name for excellent workmanship. They went on to open a briefcase loaded with cash. This was the initial deposit and further investment to deal with the cash flow problems. The cost of any alteration to the machinery or new machinery required would be made available if necessary. It was a huge contract, and the following morning, Alfred was able to explain the situation to all the employees. Their prayers had been answered, and they would not be making anyone redundant, but a few more vacancies would be made as a result of the increased workload. *"But God..."*

JOSHUA PAUL

A nother man who came with his friend was Joshua Paul. Joshua Paul was a pastor from South Korea, and his ministry was to get people to rise early in the morning to pray. He had a servant called Abu Timothy, a man from Finland. Abu Timothy attended to Joshua Paul hand and foot. He even poured his cornflakes and put the milk on them. They were a bit eccentric, but likeable.

When he travelled on the ferry, he sat in the bar, carrying a big wooden cross. No one dared enter into the bar during the crossing. Their total sales that day were for two soft drinks for Joshua Paul and Abu Timothy. When he arrived, we had a house for rent, which was unoccupied at the time, so we let them stay there. The first thing he did was place the big cross in the window, which made many people in the neighbourhood very angry and annoyed. He had been in the South Korean army and liked things done his way. I was never Donald to him, but Buchanan.

The prayer meetings were at six o'clock in the morning. For the duration of his stay, we faithfully attended those meetings and continued for a year after he left. He spoke and prayed, and you did not dare pray or do anything unless he told you to. "Buchanan, pray," he would command. If you did not attend those early morning meetings, you were considered a lazy sluggard, and every word he spoke, Abu Timothy either recorded it or wrote it down.

Very early one particular morning, I was elbowed in the ribs by Shirley. "What's that?" she said, sitting up in bed. It was twenty-to-five in the morning. She was hearing singing. We lived in a housing estate, and at times, especially at weekends, you could hear the odd wee melody as people came home from a party. "It's them," she said, "it's them!"

As I went to the window, there was Joshua Paul and his trusty servant marching up and down the street, singing at the top of their voices, "Onward Christian soldiers marching as to war." I had to get up and take them away from the housing estate as quickly as possible, for you could hear little children crying and dogs barking. The whole area was wondering what was going on. I took them in my car for their own safety and well-being. I kept driving around until it was time for the prayer meeting, which was held in Ken and Marion's home out in the country, where noise was not an issue.

DRINKING AT THE FOUNTAIN

Donnie Stewart was a pastor of a thriving Holy Ghost church on the Isle of Lewis, an island north of the Isle of Benbecula. He visited us, along with some friends, and they were full of the fire of the Holy Ghost, praying, preaching and being excited about God.

One of the stories I remember is that Donnie prayed with a young lady called Ann at the end of a meeting which was held in our home. It was about midnight, and as the power of God hit Ann, she fell prostrate on our kitchen floor. She was "slain in the Spirit" in the presence of God. Her hands were outstretched and reached towards Heaven. She was in that condition and position until after six o'clock the following morning. Such a thing is not naturally possible, but Ann was not in a natural state. She was under the supernatural, almighty, anointing power of God. And what is naturally impossible, is possible with God.

THERE WAS A THIRSTY WOMAN

Many years later, this same Ann came with us to Edinburgh for a Rodney Howard-Browne conference. She was hit by another strong anointing of the Holy Spirit, and the joy of the Lord filled her once again, with the joy breaking out as laughter. I do understand that many will not understand such a thing or believe it, but this was a situation witnessed by several people who were with us. As we left the meeting, she was like someone who was drunk: laughing and staggering. (Acts 2:15) In Edinburgh, taxis would not take 'drunk' people, and trying to explain that Ann was drunk in the Spirit (and not with alcohol) would not have been an easy exercise.

We were staying in a flat rented by Ann's sister and a friend, who were both going to be away for a few days (although the friend agreed to meet us before leaving). By the time we got there, the anointing had also come upon a lady called Marion Reece and upon Shirley, so they were like the three musketeers, all laughing. Ann's boyfriend, Paul, had great concerns about Ann's well-being.

Upon arrival we were met by a lovely young lady. Being the only sensible person, I addressed her, trying to explain the situation as best as I could. However, I suspected that she thought we were a bunch of idiots, or even weirdos! I asked her if she was a Christian girl, and she replied that she went to church sometimes. This young lady was about twenty-one years old, She told me that she was broken-hearted, as her relationship with her boyfriend had recently broken up.

The three musketeers, now sitting on the settee, laughed again. When she went on to tell me she was planning suicide, they laughed louder, and the situation was like a bad comedy. This young lady explained that she was a third-year medical student and knew exactly how to kill herself. She told me that her family had failed her, and I again heard laughter. Her father had abused her, while her mother refused to believe her, and her brother sided with her father. She felt alone in this big world. The laughter continued, and at the end, in my desperation, I suggested that I pray for her.

At this moment, the atmosphere changed. There was a cessation as if a conductor had brought the orchestra to the end of a symphony. Silence reigned. A short prayer later, our new-found friend (who was leaving the building and heading out into the world with plans in her head to kill herself) now had a simple prayer accompanying her on her journey. Whatever happened through that simple prayer, only God really knows. But God appears to have moved into her life. We heard that some years later she had a professional job as a doctor, was happily married and enjoying life.

I believe that without this almost comical situation, which I cannot explain or understand, the circumstances would have been very different. God's ways are past finding out - another *"But God..."* moment.

HOLY LAUGHTER

Although I have given an account of the phenomena they call "Holy Laughter," it was an experience we had encountered several times in our meetings, especially the house meetings. Mature men and women would laugh in absolute freedom as a springing up of joy from their innermost being came to the surface. Some would be on all fours on the floor, while others lay face down, and this joy would, at times, be infectious. Some would pretend it was happening to them, but the difference between the real thing and that manufactured from the flesh was blatantly obvious.

We were witnesses to people being set free from depression and other issues by these amazing encounters with the Lord. We understand that people spoke negatively about these experiences, which were happening in many churches worldwide. However, when you experienced it first-hand, you could not question that this was simply the overwhelming fruit of the Spirit of joy setting people free and bringing freedom and life back to the Body of Christ.

HEARING FROM GOD

Ann, (mentioned earlier), was married to Paul in 1996. Paul was from Inverness, and they met in the hallway of our home. It was love at first sight. Paul was a young man hungry for God. In May of the following year, Paul and I took three days out to seek God in the moorlands behind the largest hill in Benbecula, which is just over four hundred feet above sea level. This was during the days just before the election that saw Tony Blair elected as Prime Minister (May 1997).

We stayed in a small tent, and in the same dress code as on the day we were born, we plunged into a cold Hebridean loch in the morning to wash ourselves and wake ourselves up. We then spent the days praying, reading the Bible, walking and talking, and seeking God. On the third day, we were disappointed that the encounter we wanted with God had not materialised and that we had simply wasted our time. Climbing to the top of the hill called Rueval, I knelt down to pray, repenting of any sin in my life. I told the Lord that unless I was going to be purposeful for the sake of the Gospel, I wanted to die there and then. As I prayed and cried to God, I began to weep. As I did so, I heard an inner voice that said, 'I shall not die, but live, and declare the works of the Lord.'

It was later, as I spoke to Shirley, that I realised this was a verse in the Scriptures. It is found in Psalm 118:17. For the first time in my life, I had heard the voice of the Lord so clearly that it was as if it had been audible. It was quiet but came with authority, and I praise God that is an experience I have enjoyed on several occasions over the years.

Since that time, I have heard the voice of the Lord directing me on several occasions. At one time, I was at a certain place and saw a man in the distance. He was prominent in Christian circles, although I did not know him very well. He also visited the South of Ireland regularly. As I had sixty euros in my wallet, I thought I would give that money to him, as we had no plans to go abroad or to the South in the near future. He was standing approximately one hundred yards from me, and I took the cash out of my wallet to have it ready when I believe I heard the Lord speak to me and say, "Do not give that man your money; he is not the man you think he is."

Shocked and surprised, I held on to my money, and by the time I got home to tell Shirley, I was questioning whether I had heard from the Lord. Sometime later, there was a situation, and the very man I had planned to give the money to was exposed for a very serious crime.

A different situation took place in the Elim Church at Dungannon. I was not preaching anywhere on that Sunday evening, and I thought I would go and fellowship with the folk at that church, as they are a lovely group of Godly people. We had visited a few people on our journey there. I needed to use the toilet, and there in that toilet, the Lord spoke to me to prepare myself to preach, as the speaker they had booked for the evening would not be turning up.

Again, I told Shirley what I believed I had heard, and sure enough, the speaker did not turn up. Noel, the elder there, asked me to share something. In the short time before I was called up to preach, God had prepared a Word in my heart.

HUGH BLACK

In Benbecula, we met up with Pauline Anderson, a pretty young lady with a message from God. She was from a church called Struthers Memorial Church in Glasgow, and we later learned that there were several of those churches planted in various places in the United Kingdom.

Pauline spoke about her pastor with fondness, and I was to learn that he was none other than Hugh Black, whom I had heard about. Hugh had written several books and was well-known in certain circles in the Scottish Highlands and Islands. Pauline told me of a conference that the church was having at Wiston Lodge in Lanarkshire and asked if I would like to go. At that time, I would be in the Normandy Hotel in Paisley, attending a training conference with Pearl Assurance. Pauline said she would pick me up and take me back there. I was excited about the possibility of meeting Hugh Black, as he was (to me) someone famous.

That lunchtime, a message came through to me that Pauline was sorry that she could not collect me, as something had come up. I was a little disappointed, but it was not a major issue. The day's training was over, and as I settled, preparing for dinner, a call came to my room: "Mr. Buchanan, there is a gentleman at reception asking to see you." As I went down to reception, there was this big man. Big in size and big in personality. I would now say big in God. He had come to collect me, driving through Paisley in rush-hour traffic. He did all that for me. I felt very important and encouraged in the Lord.

As the evening meeting began, a lady came onto the platform. I was later told it was Mr. Black's daughter, either Grace or Mary. She spoke with a deep Glasgow accent but with thundering authority. "You are here tonight," she said. "You are here uninvited. You did not come of your own free will. You have been sent," she continued. The silence in the hall was deafening. "You have placed your thresholds beside my threshold, your posts beside my posts (see Ezekiel 43:8), says the Lord, but you are not here for the right reasons." I thought she was referring to me, and I was searching my heart when three people stood up and walked out in a hurry.

Later, I was told they had been sent from the local witches' coven. As the meeting went on, Hugh Black preached God's Word, and I thought, "Lord, I want that man to pray over me, lay hands on me and anoint me." It was as if there was a time warp, and behind me, what seemed like immediately, I heard this person praying in tongues. As this person laid hands on me, I began to understand that this was Hugh Black. I felt the wonderful anointing of the Holy Spirit move over me and through me, and I began to feel so blessed as he had walked through a crowd of people to pray for me. As far as I know, he did not pray for anyone else that evening. As I whispered to the Lord to thank Him, I felt very special. I felt like a man called of God.

DENIS GOODELL

Denis Goodell was an American ex-serviceman who had been to Vietnam. He told how he was in charge of two hundred and fifty-five young soldiers in Vietnam, and at the end of his time, only five had survived. He had many stories, such as hiding in a pit of snakes and praying that God would protect him while the Vietcong searched for him. He was wounded in Vietnam and lost his leg. Every day, he lost a cup full of blood from a wound. Not being able to exercise, he weighed over thirty stones. He did carry a mighty anointing, and we were happy to have him visit us.

He told us not to come near him when he slept, as his reaction could be to lash out to defend himself due to flashbacks from the Vietnam war. He told us that with one move, he could kill a man and we should stay well away when he slept. I remember one day he did fall asleep in a chair in a neighbour's living room, and every neighbour from all around came to look at this man, fearful of going too near him, in case they got killed. With joy, I go on record to say we all survived his visit! During his visit, however, many were touched and blessed by the Lord. Denis sat in a chair during the meeting, and those who went to be prayed for were either "slain in the Spirit" or had some other visible encounter with the Holy Ghost.

PAUL HAUFMAN

Another interesting character who came to visit was a man called Paul Haufman. He was also a Vietnam veteran and an ex-military officer who was used to ordering people about. He must have been about six foot ten inches tall and often demanded a flannel (which was a damp cloth) to wipe his hands. His personality and character were, at best, questionable, as he came across as cold-hearted and uncaring. But he carried a mighty Holy Ghost anointing, so you had to give him some leeway and respect.

I took Paul up to Stornoway (revival country) to do some meetings. Upon arrival at the home of the pastor, Catriona (the pastor's wife) had a lovely dinner ready for him. When we asked him to present himself at the table, he decided he was fasting but wanted a flannel. Catriona shared his dinner with the others at the table, so off we went to the meeting shortly afterwards. At the meeting, he preached a great Word, and then the Holy Spirit moved in power as people were healed and Baptised in the Holy Spirit.

One of these people was my own son, David, who was drunk in the Spirit for three days afterwards. He, too, carried an anointing, and whenever he prayed for people, God's power was released, and mighty things happened. That evening, we took Paul back to the pastor's home, where he began to demand his dinner, but the pot was empty. The dinner was long gone, so he had to fill his belly with bread and jam sandwiches. A few days later, he was leaving, and this tall man was demanding that Mina (Shirley's mother, who stood at five foot and half an inch) carry his suitcases. I do not know what she said to him, but some days later, we received a letter of apology from him for his lack of respect and manners!

STRENGTHENING FAITH

I remember taking David (my son) on a journey to the Isle of Lewis for a faith-building exercise. I knew that there was a caravan park where you could rent a caravan for a night or a few days. But the object of this faith-building exercise was to prove to David that God will supply our needs.

We did not book any accommodation because we prayed God would open doors and we would have a breakfast every morning. One of our stops on the first day was with Donald Saunders (whom we previously mentioned). After being in his house for a short time, he inquired as to where we were staying. I said, "We have a plan" (which I had in the back of my mind). "You will stay here," he demanded. "I am here alone and would love your company. My daughter called yesterday and changed the two single beds in the back room." I looked at David, smiling. God had provided.

The following days, after breakfast, we called to see Donald MacPhail. Donald was the young man mentioned in the books written about the Lewis Revival. He was the sixteen-year-old who sat in the window of the church when Duncan Campbell asked him to pray. He began his prayer by addressing God as Father. His prayer brought heaven down. Donald was now an elderly man, and we reminisced with stories about days of old. "Will you stay with me tonight?" he asked. "Morag (his wife) has gone down to Edinburgh for a few days," he continued, "and she just changed the beds in case anyone called to stay." Pretending to be reluctant, we agreed to stay with him. We enjoyed his fellowship, a great night's sleep, and breakfast in the morning.

The next day was Sunday, and we fellowshipped with New Wine Church in Stornoway. After some lunch, we headed down the long road to Leverburgh in the South of Harris, passing Tarbert as we did so. I had now proven to David that God provides our needs, so the point was made. I was prepared to pay for bed and breakfast in Leverburgh, as we had to get a ferry back at 6.30am.

In Leverburgh, the majority of the bed and breakfast owners are very religious Sabbath observants, who do not take bed and breakfast on a Sunday night. We had an estate car and considered sleeping in the car, but David did not show any enthusiasm for that idea. It was now late afternoon, and to pass the time, we decided to go back to Tarbert and visit dear friends called Angus Alick and Ina. Knowing that they did bed and breakfast, we were not going to ask them to give us a room, as we thought they would not take any payment and we would be "using" them.

As we pulled up to their house, Ina came out to welcome us. Soon, Angus Alick came inside to see us, and the welcome was warm and sincere. "Oh, Donald Buchanan, how good to see you," they said. "Are you the two the Lord has sent to stay here tonight?" "You see," she said, "I have been fully booked all season, and today I got a phone- call from a couple who had booked some time ago. I only had the twin room, but they were happy with that. Today, they phoned me and told me they were in the wrong Tarbert. They were in Tarbert, Loch Fyne, and we are here in Tarbert, Harris, and they cannot get here as the ferry did not run on the Sunday."

She convinced us that this was the Lord's doing, and graciously, we accepted a blessing from the Lord. Angus Alick and Ina provided all our needs that evening, but the hand of God was clearly being seen by David and me. The next day, we returned home, knowing another of God's promises being fulfilled.

David has gone on to serve God with Perth Christian Fellowship, and has now moved to the Scottish Highlands, where we believe God will use him mightily. At the time of writing, David has four children: Faith, Hannah, Zoe, and Elijah, with one on the way. He is married to Jenni.

DEE'S BIG DECISIONS

Deirdre, our daughter, had several experiences with God as a young girl, but at the age of eighteen, there were various things pulling at her life. We refused to restrain her and gave her free will, but also gave her Godly advice. We told her never to go to the Junior Ranks club in the Army Camp as she would get a bad reputation. Although we would have preferred her not to get involved in the social life in Benbecula (which was centred around pubs and drinking), she was at an age where she had to make up her own mind. Certain people tried very hard to lead her astray, but God was bigger and stronger, and He kept her.

I recall her big decision regarding the choice whether to follow the Lord or the ways of the world. She was in her bedroom praying, and when she came downstairs, she explained that she had come to a decision. In fear and trepidation, we awaited this decision. To the praises of the Lord, her decision was to follow the ways of the Lord.

A few years later, there was another big decision to be made, as God had a calling on her life. It was to leave the safety of island life, and commit herself to train and to serve with Youth for Christ. That decision was also a positive one, and after training in Coventry, she was posted to Glasgow for a while, later returning to Coventry to oversee the Youth for Christ Academy. From there, she went to work with Christ for all Nations (Reinhard Bonnke's ministry). Today, she is married to an Elim pastor called Simon, and they are successfully planting a church in Wolverhampton. Deirdre (or Dee as she is now known to many) is the mother of two lovely children, Cara and Evie.

The Life City Church, which Simon and Dee have planted, offers space within the building for various events, especially charity events. A lady who was running a charity event had some helpers with her. One of these people was her sister, and Deirdre engaged with her in a short conversation. Several months later, Deirdre met the same lady again in Wolverhampton city centre, and remembering her from the charity event, they again engaged in small talk (as this lady had recently become a grandmother). Deirdre commented on how well she looked and gave some encouraging, warm words, not fully knowing what was going on in the background.

Sometime later, this woman attended the church a few times and got saved. On the day of her baptism, part of her testimony was how that day, when Deirdre spoke to her, she was at an all-time low and making plans to commit suicide. Those friendly words of blessing changed her whole life and has influenced the life of others along the journey.

THE NIGHT WE MET A WITCH

As time went on, we were being invited to many new places to preach and encourage churches. When we visited Northern Ireland, Shirley's mother would have a full itinerary of engagements waiting for us, from women's meetings to churches and fellowships. We were blessed. We got to know people like John and Doreen Greenaway and the folk at the River of Life church, where we experienced mighty touches of the Holy Ghost.

Although we had met Jimmy Winning some years previously, Jimmy wanted us to learn and understand more about the ministry he was involved with. His calling was to the ministries of healing and deliverance. He explained that demonic forces can affect people's health and well-being, as well as their finances and many other areas of their lives. Demonic forces can influence family situations, even down through generational lines. Involvement in certain organisations like the Freemasons, and especially the oaths people make and take, can be detrimental to the whole family. Things like curses can affect homes, farms, businesses and families, but after these curses are broken in the name of Jesus, individuals, families, and businesses will be blessed and prosper.

We would stay at the Annaghanoon Christian Ministry's flat for several nights, working with Jimmy and his friend Robin. One evening during our training, a Christian lady we knew brought her friend for prayer. As soon as this friend came through the door, a thought crossed our minds: that thought said, "WITCH!" As we proceeded to inquire about her needs, she told us she had a sore shoulder, but the Holy Spirit continued to prompt us about this witch situation. I finally said that we could pray for her, but there was a situation regarding witchcraft which needed addressing. She denied all knowledge of what we were talking about, telling us that she was a good Christian woman. Her friend confirmed this statement.

Still, we were persuaded to pursue the matter, asking her if her parents had dabbled in the occult or had she ever used the Ouija board, tarot cards, or anything like that. She replied "no" to every question. We began to see a pattern in her replies. A "yes" was "I can't say," and a "no" was a "no." After a gruelling time of interrogation, she finally admitted that she was a witch. At this point, her friend nearly fainted! This woman went to church every Sunday. Although Jimmy was with us, he had not involved himself with the situation up to this point. Realising that she had now confessed her real involvement in witchcraft, I cried out, "Jimmy, Jimmy, she's a witch!"

Jimmy questioned her about being initiated into witchcraft and her assignments, etc. She reluctantly admitted that her assignment was to pray for the break-up of Christian marriages. She attended church every Sunday, as well as every prayer meeting, where she heard about the struggles that go on in different homes (especially people going through marriage problems). When they were leaving, Jimmy asked her friend to go into her house when she took her home.

We learned later that her reason for the visit was to find out about Shirley and I. Her friend went home with her and came back about twenty minutes later, accompanied by her husband. She was shouting, "Jimmy, Donald, Shirley!" She had taken the woman back home to her house, and in the lady's living room were two coffins. There was one on each side of the fireplace and a chair that had come from an Egyptian tomb, which would have been worth an absolute fortune. This lady was on benefits from the government but doing the work of the devil. This was our first real encounter with the "wiles of the devil" at that level. Her assignment was to pray for the break-up of Christian marriages, but understanding that such a person could be found in a church (which would preach and teach the whole counsel of God) opened our eyes to the capability of the devil to blind us to his ways.

Whilst I was working and learning from Jimmy, he explained that when someone has a demon in them, you have authority in Jesus' name to cast that demon out and set the people free. That demon can cause the person to cough, sneeze, or even be sick when leaving. They can also scream or shout. They may weep, but there will often be a manifestation coming through an orifice in the body. On rare occasions, this manifestation can be through the passing of wind from the lower part of the body, which can be very embarrassing. One lady who came for prayer had an angry spirit, which we ministered into. Some young people had left the room, sitting on the upper part of the stairs. The means by which this angry spirit left was by the passing of wind. The lady went into the hall, embarrassed by her predicament and let loose some special explosions, not knowing that the young people were on the stairs! After it was all over, we sat down and had a wonderful time sharing the funny side of the situation! The lady was set free and now enjoys life in all its fullness.

JIMMY WINNING

These two instances, as well as others, were part of our training in the ministry of deliverance under the watchful eye of Jimmy Winning. Many years previously, Jimmy had joined a prayer line at a meeting in Stevenson in Ayrshire, Scotland. The man ministering had a Word from the Lord for him. "The Lord is calling you into a ministry where he will use you to bring healing and help to many. It is called the ministry of deliverance. It is not a ministry that will make you popular with many other believers. It is, however, a ministry that is from the hand of God, and should you accept this calling before this day is over, the Lord will anoint you with the power and authority for this ministry." In his heart, Jimmy said, "Yes" to the Lord.

On his way home from the meeting, at about 10pm, he saw a big lady with two children walking the road. It was pouring with rain, and they were soaking wet as Jimmy stopped to give them a lift in his small van. Jimmy asked what the problem was, and she told him that her husband had come home drunk. She then came out with the following sentence, which was like music to Jimmy's ears: "That man has got a devil in him," she said. Immediately, the words of the preacher rang in Jimmy's ear. "Before this day is over," was what was said, and this was Jimmy's opportunity to find out if the authority and the power were there for him to operate in this ministry.

Jimmy knew the man, and after dropping the woman and the children off at his home for his wife to help them, he proceeded to go and see her husband. The man was very drunk, hallucinating and seeing little men with bowler hats walking around on the worktops in the kitchen. It was Jimmy's opportunity. Praying for a drunk man is never easy, but praying for one who is having *Delirium Tremens* is almost impossible. As the man kept on telling Jimmy about the little men with the bowler hats, he imagined one falling into a basin in the sink. Removing the basin and placing it on the floor, he dived in to rescue the tiny, imagined person. In this rescue mission, he banged his head against the cupboard door, knocking himself out. Jimmy was left looking at this poor soul "out cold" on the kitchen floor, lying there in a drunken stupor. Jimmy's analysis of the situation was that his ministry of deliverance could not be exercised to a man in this condition. He made the man comfortable and safe, threw a blanket over him and left, feeling unable to help.

Heading home, he was disappointed that he had failed the Lord, and arriving home, it was now almost midnight. Entering the kitchen, the lady he had given the lift to inquired about her husband and what Jimmy expected to do to help him. Jimmy told her the story of the meeting and the ministry he felt called to. "I was going to pray for your husband, Missus, and cast a demon out of him. Immediately, this woman attacked him, knocked him to the ground, and sat on top of him. She grabbed him by the throat, stopping him from breathing. As already said, she was a big lady, and Jimmy fought to get her hand removed from his throat. As he did so, he called out, "JESUS!" The woman immediately stood up and helped Jimmy onto his feet without any recollection of what had happened. It was the woman who had the demon, and upon calling the name of Jesus, she was delivered and set free. Jimmy looked at his watch, and it was five minutes to midnight.

As the prophecy said: "Before this day is over, the Lord will anoint you with the power and authority for this ministry." Jimmy went on to move to Northern Ireland, helping many people, setting many free from demonic spiritual oppression and influences, and leading many people to Jesus for salvation and healing.

A CHANGE OF LIFE

In 1998, Shirley had a serious accident at work. She suffered a head injury and was like someone who had been struck down with a stroke. She had difficulty walking and speaking and was very weak. It was diagnosed as Cerebellar Syndrome, which is basically damage to the nervous system in the brain area at the back of the head. It was very debilitating, and in the first initial moments after the accident, she was paralysed from the waist downwards.

Within the first few days, feeling came back to her legs and feet, and I remember telling the Lord that whatever the situation was going to be, that with His help, we would pull through. At this time, the Fellowship numbers had also dwindled, as the Ministry of Defence was cutting back in the islands, and many of the servicemen and their families had been posted out to other military bases. We had never really been well supported by the locals in Benbecula. However, some did visit now and again, attending if we had something special happening or a special preacher or speaker coming to hold meetings.

For the next two years, Shirley was my main cause for concern. There were days of frustration and days of tears as she struggled to gain her health back. In those times, our son David and our daughter Deirdre were such an inspiration and encouragement (as were others, especially a lady called Cindy, the wife of Mervyn, an RAF serviceman stationed in Benbecula). Some days, when Shirley felt at rock bottom, Deirdre would take her hand and pray for her. There would be like an immediate enabling and empowering, and Shirley would be up, ready to go out.

We bought a metal detector to encourage her and give her a reason to go out, but should the detector pick up a signal from below ground that there was some object, I was left to do the digging. "Dig, dig," was the command, and I had to go on my hands and knees until an old rusty bolt or tin can was recovered.

One night, at a meeting we had in the Steading, at Nunton, Benbecula, Shirley went forward for prayer. Donald Saunders and I prayed for her. When we had finished praying, she told the other Donald that when he had put his hand on her head, she sensed a power go through her body. Neither Donald nor I had placed our hand on Shirley's head, which she found hard to believe, for she said that someone had placed a hand on her head. From that night, Shirley's recovery quickened, and soon, she was in a position to continue her life more or less as normal. However, there were some situations she was best to avoid, like places where there was too much noise or too much activity.

After Shirley's recovery, with also the numbers attending the meetings having dwindled significantly, we felt that the Lord was going to move us on. We were still very active in ministry, with people coming from mainland Scotland for prayer and help. Under Jimmy Winning's teaching, we had learned many interesting things about deliverance. We also studied some of Derek Prince's teachings. Although most churches (including those who call themselves Pentecostal) do not believe in or accept this ministry, we believe it was still very real and very relevant. We believe this because of the many people we were able to help and set free from all kinds of physical and mental illnesses, including deliverance from serious cases such as suicidal tendencies and self-harming.

THE GOD OF RESTORATION

Many years later, in the midst of all that was going on, I managed to restore my relationship with my father and mother. I was also able to be reconciled with the rest of my family, although sharing my faith with them could still be a little contentious. Before my parents passed away, I was privileged to share my faith with them. I was able to share what I believe with my father over a period of time. My father had a depth to his faith outwith (over and above) the ritual and ceremony of Catholicism. He would sometimes ask me to pray for him regarding ailments and pains he suffered as he got older.

The following day, he would tell me my prayers did not work, and we would laugh about it together. His thoughts on God were simple and prayerful. Late at night, he would turn in his chair onto his knees and pray. It did not matter who was in the house, but this was him being thankful to God. For the following minutes, groaning and utterings were heard as he reached out to God. My mother was extremely Catholic. You would say a staunch Catholic. She was a very kind lady whose religion was rooted in ritual and centred on the attending of mass, along with showing kindness and generosity to others. Later in life, she would take small strokes (I think they called them T.I.A.s), and then one day, a major stroke affected her so severely, she was taken to hospital.

I went to see her ten days before she died, almost desperate to share Jesus with her. She had made a slight recovery and was able to speak, although she was badly affected by the stroke and was very weak. I gently asked her that if she should die, did she have confidence to say that she would go to Heaven. "How can anyone know that Donald?" she inquired. Here was this lovely lady who had led a life faithful to her beliefs with no assurance of her eternal destiny.

I explained the Holy Scriptures to her, of how Jesus had died for sinners. I told her how that simply on our acceptance of His sacrificial offering of Himself in dying for us, and by believing this and trusting Him, we could have eternal salvation. I asked if she would pray a small prayer with me, and with eyes looking straight at me, she said, "Yes, that would be good." As we prayed, I pointed her to Jesus, knowing that there was no other name under Heaven by which she could be saved from the judgement of God. I knew that being a Catholic or a Protestant was never going to suffice a Holy God, Who had given His dear and only begotten Son, Jesus, as a sacrifice for sin: accepting Jesus as our Saviour is God's only way of salvation. That day, a transaction took place between my mother and God which, I am confident secured her eternal destiny.

JEHOVAH JIREH

As the military houses emptied of army and RAF personnel, there were rumours on the island that the Ministry of Defence was going to knock all the military houses down. It was said that this was in the contract of agreement signed many years previously. Believing that these houses were in good condition, I made inquiries on behalf of others, asking if they would consider selling them rather than razing them to the ground.

There was one section of the housing estate with eighteen houses, and we learned that they would sell them on condition that all the houses in that section were sold. Informing some of the young families on the island of the prospect of getting a bargain, we negotiated for a deal. The houses at the time were valued at about twenty thousand pounds. We offered three thousand for three-bedroom houses and two and a half thousand for two-bedroom houses.

I had already bought my council house at a discounted price, so I had negotiated for the others, and we made the offer through solicitors. To our joy, the Ministry of Defence accepted our offer. Unfortunately, at the last moment, a man who planned on buying two of the three-bedroom houses pulled out of the deal, leaving us all "snookered." I knocked on doors to try and find other buyers, but to no avail.

Eventually, Shirley and I bought both houses, one for three thousand pounds. We further negotiated the second for six hundred pounds to allow the deal to go through. The second house had been broken into and flooded, which was the reason for the low price. As DIY enthusiasts, Shirley and I began to clearing, cleaning up and painting. Our children helped when they could.

Soon, one house was ready, and we offered it as a place for a free holiday to anyone in full-time Christian work. When the second one was ready, a couple came to our door asking to rent the property, and soon, we were bringing in finances we had never dreamed of. Within a short time, both houses were rented out, and we were receiving a regular income. Somehow, before the age of fifty (twenty years after being in total despair due to debt), we were in a position to give up work and were entertaining the thought of going into full-time Christian work.

A PROMISE MADE BEFORE GOD

After Shirley's healing, we felt a prompting that God was going to move us on. Shirley and I had been married for twenty-five years, and she had spent all her married life confined to a small island. She told me that if she had killed me on the wedding night and pleaded guilty to the offence, she would be out of prison by now! (I think she was joking!) We set our hearts to pray, telling the Lord that whatever He had for us, we wanted to simply be obedient and serve Him.

I also made a promise to Shirley that by the time I was fifty years old, we would not be living on the island. We had our dear friend Carol Anderson (Arlow) witness that promise.

THE PROPHET SAID: "THE MOVE IS ON"

As time passed, I was being invited to preach at meetings on the mainland. Although I loved the challenge of new places, the travelling and the cost was a bit of a hardship. I had to take the ferry from North Uist to the Isle of Skye (two hours) and drive wherever the meetings were held.

On a certain occasion, I had managed to get back to the Isle of Skye on a Saturday afternoon. I was delighted to hear that a certain man named Howard Chiplin, a recognised prophet in the Apostolic Church, was going to be present. That Saturday evening at a house meeting, I met this lovely man, and the following morning at the church meeting, he pointed at me and said, "Do it. Just do it." Immediately, I understood what he meant. It was the move we were praying about. But as I pondered these words, he continued: "You do not know me, and therefore, you may doubt that this is God's Word for you. But the Lord has spoken to your wife (on a natural level, he did not even know I had a wife), and He has told her that the month to do it is September. When you phone her, she will confirm September, and that will confirm that this is of the Lord."

In those days (April 2003), there were very few mobile phones. Some would have a brick-sized phone in their car, but the old telephone kiosk was still the order of the day regarding phone calls. After finding a phone box, I phoned Shirley. I told her the story about the man and what he had said. I told her he had told me that she would know which month. "Yes," she said, "as I prayed, the Lord spoke to me and told me the month was September." On the 30th of September 2003, Shirley and I had a Ford Sierra Estate car filled to capacity and left this beautiful little island called Benbecula on another adventure with God. Whether we are ever to return, we do not know.

LEAVING BENBECULA WITH MEMORIES

As we left Benbecula in September 2003, feeling a lot like Abraham (as we did not know where we were going), we took with us fond memories and remembrances of wonderful, unforgettable experiences and wonderful people. As a result of God's provision, we were able to retire from secular work and commit our time to serving the Lord.

Those memories were often of experiences with friends like Marion Reece. We recalled praying over the phone with her for healing concerning her backache, which she had suffered for years. God touched her and healed her. Marion recently told me that her back problems never came back. Marion was also blessed with a "Word of knowledge" from Michael Backholer, regarding her mother. This man, not knowing her concern for her mother's eternal security, was told that her mother was safe with Jesus and she would see her again. This moment has been etched on Marion's life ever since and has given her a peace regarding her mother's salvation.

Marion was also one (along with others) who fellowshipped with us one night in our home. Whilst worshipping and praising the Lord, a strong wind blew in through the living room. Some felt it, but others didn't. I am privileged to say that I was one of the people who did feel that phenomenon on that evening. All the doors and windows were closed, and we have to believe that it was simply another *"But God"* moment.

Jim and Sheena Lynch also heard and saw God operate in his glorious power. My memory is cast back to the time when Sheena was hospitalised, but was not making any progress. At that time, we had a series of special meetings. Jim was getting a little fed up with the medical profession and signed his wife out of hospital. He brought her to a meeting where she was gloriously healed. The ambulance driver (who had taken Sheena to the hospital) saw her the next day and was astounded at her condition and fullness of health. Sheena's daughter, Kim, walked into a meeting one night with crutches and walked out, leaving her crutches behind her, totally healed.

We had Harry Sprange, a Baptist minister with a well-known youth ministry, visit the island to encourage the young ones in the Fellowship. There would have been upwards of twenty who came to a meeting where Harry would speak. As they gathered in the home of Miss Chris Day, an army captain, things did not go as planned. A young man called Karl, who was 15 years old at the time, stood up to speak. As he shared God's Word, there were tears and weeping as the Holy Spirit took over the meeting, touching all those young ones, bringing healing and restoration to them in spirit, soul and body. We are still waiting for Harry's encouraging words of wisdom.

There were stories, such as Chrissie Meeks, who told us that she was suffering from insomnia whilst she was pregnant, and as we prayed for her, she fell asleep. We had to carry her home, where she slept until well into the afternoon of the following day. How can we ever forget Carol Arlow (now Carol Anderson)? What a woman of faith. She was our means of encouragement on so many occasions through so many hard but interesting times. Her children's work and stories about her pet lamb (called Lamborghini) were an inspiration to us all.

OVER THE SEA TO SKYE

The day we left Benbecula, there was sadness and excitement. We crossed over on the ferry to Skye. Alasdair Matheson and Barbara, his wife, were good friends living on the Isle of Skye. They had five lovely children. Alasdair was the pastor of Skye Bible Church, and he had stayed with us when he was teaching in Benbecula. With no plans as to where we should go, they gave us a bedroom to use as our own. We believed that this room was going to be like Jesus' grave, only for use as a short-term residency! We did not believe that this was our final abode and that doors would open for us to serve the Lord.

For the next three weeks, we were stuck in that bedroom. We did not preach or pray for anyone, and began to wonder if we had made the right move or a dreadful mistake. Then, unexpectedly, we got a call from a man called Sandy Sutherland, an elder in the Free Church of Scotland in Lairg. He asked if I would come to preach in the church, as their minister had left, and they had no preacher.

Well, it was better than nothing, as far as I was concerned, although the Free Church would not be one of my favourite denominations! I was a Pentecostal with a strong conviction of the need of the work of the Holy Spirit, and would therefore have to show constraint about my beliefs. I thought that some of the ministers I had known from that denomination were aloof and had a superior attitude. They claim to be Bible-believing (as I would also), but our understanding of the Scriptures would differ in many ways.

We would differ regarding the teaching of the Baptism of the Holy Spirit and the gifts of the Spirit. We would differ also in our understanding of water baptism. They would baptise children (which I believe to be a Roman Catholic Church teaching that is not Scriptural). I would have to fit in with the Free Church theology, but in order to win souls for Jesus, I was prepared to do whatever it took, as long as it was not immoral or illegal. The church is strongly Calvinist but I am not (although I do understand their point of view on this matter).

I once spoke to a gentleman, and as I witnessed to him and asked him to consider Christ, he told me that if he was one of the elect then he would be saved. If not, then he would not be saved, and there was nothing he could do about it. I understand the teaching of Calvinism, but this man's understanding was too severe for me to comprehend.

After praying about accepting the invitation to Lairg, we began to see it as an open door of opportunity, rather than viewing it in a negative way. With all that said, I must add that the vast majority of the congregations I have known and worked with have been really lovely, God-fearing, people. Having accepted this invitation, we were privileged to have preached in Free Churches in Lairg, Rogart, Golspie, Dornoch, Brora and Lochinver, where we met and made friends with believers and non-believers.

FREE CHURCH, LAIRG

In Lairg, we met up with Sandy and Angela and immediately recognised a kindred spirit. Sandy was the leading elder, and his heart, like that of his wife, was after God. The other elder was the late Hector MacLennan, who was married to Margaret. These four were the stalwarts of the church. They had about twenty people coming to the morning meetings and about twelve to the evening services. The prayer meeting was also poorly attended.

As I met the people, we found them lovely and warm, and my heart went out to them. They were like sheep without a shepherd. Some were open to the things of the Spirit but had to hide it. After the first Sunday, when all went well, we were invited back for a three-month period. We stayed in the Manse, which they were updating, and we loved it. We had folks round for dinner and got to know the core of the people. On visiting some of them, they gave testimonies of their salvation, but believed they were not good enough to go to the Lord's Table (known also as Communion).

With encouragement and explanation of the Holy Scriptures, the next Communion season saw some six or more going forward to the Lord's Table and becoming members of the church. Working alongside Sandy and the others, we were making inroads into the community, and every week, extra people would come along. After the three-month period, we had to leave, but came back again a few months later. The increase continued until there were fifty to sixty regulars at the morning meeting. The evening meeting was attended by over thirty to forty people, many of them having travelled far and wide to be there. One lady travelled from Dunbeath to attend Sunday evening meetings (a round trip distance of one hundred miles).

What was the attraction? Was it a good preacher or great singers? No, none of these things. It was the manifest presence of the Holy

Spirit and, consequently, men and women who believed for more of God.

The Sunday evening meeting was like a touch from Heaven, with tears flowing, as Jesus penetrated His healing power into hearts and revived their souls. On one occasion, at a special family service, over one hundred people came to the church. Some commented that they had never before seen that number of people attending (with the exception of weddings or funerals). It was rumoured that those in authority were showing concerns that this church in Lairg was being blessed, yet there was no Free Church minister in authority. Some would say that jealousy was creeping in (as can be the case in any church or situation where the hands of humanity are involved). The work of the devil is never far away when God's people are being blessed and encouraged.

One Sunday evening, I was asked to address the young people in a small room off the church hall. I explained the Gospel, and three of them were already believers. There were eighteen in all. After a short talk, I asked how many of them would like to give their hearts to Jesus. Except for the three who were already saved, every hand went up. Thinking that Sandy the elder would not believe me if I continued into repentance and a sinner's prayer situation, I went to find him and brought him back to the room. I went over the situation again, explaining the difficulties of being a Christian, and in every way, tried to make tem aware of the cost , but they would have none of it. Eventually, two said they would like to think more about it, but every other young person repented of their sin and asked Jesus to come into their hearts and save them.

Sandy and Hector were responsible for the day to day running of the church. Sandy was also responsible for choosing the speakers and preachers. Some of the hierarchy in the denomination were concerned about his choice of preachers. I had never really worked with a denomination before and am told there can be power struggles and church politics operating in the background of various churches, including the Free Church. They removed Sandy's authority to appoint speakers. Those who were now commissioned to do so chose retired Free Church ministers and elders from other churches in the denomination to conduct the services. They brought back a form of Godliness, but soon, the manifold Presence of God that had been enjoyed in the prayer meetings and Sunday services was gone. Soon, a small group of believers felt they were forced to leave that church and founded Lairg Christian Fellowship, which, I am pleased to report, is a light in the midst of much religious darkness.

FREE CHURCH, ROGART

Having encouraged the church at Lairg, we were invited to Rogart Free Church by another Sandy Sutherland. We "renamed" the two men as Sandy Lairg and Sandy Rogart. Again, the people in the congregation were lovely, warm and friendly, but we had come with a warning notice: we were classified as dangerous as we did not agree with Free Church theology (which I have previously mentioned). More church politics were also going on in the background at Rogart. The people loved us, but again, some of the hierarchy wanted us out, although they feared the opinion of the congregation.

Often, on a Monday morning, a Volvo 740 would park outside the Manse in which we were staying. A minister (who was the overseer of the church at Rogart) would come in, having received a complaint about my theology or doctrine. This minister was very laid back, and we liked him. He was simply making sure that he was attending to the complaint or complaints he had received. Life as a travelling preacher man is not easy, especially when you are required to stay within a certain framework of teaching that you find difficult to accept. But, due to the call of Christ, you must endure such trials.

We took a choir from Perth Christian Fellowship to Rogart at one time, and they were amazing. Crowds came to hear them, and the place was packed out. Sandy Rogart would say that Donald and Shirley had put Rogart on the map as a result of this wonderful night, which was the talking point of the village and the surrounding villages for many weeks. Sandy sadly passed away a few years ago and will be fondly remembered.

Shirley and I loved the people and never considered the denomination of any "church" we worked with. One certain minister had a bit of an issue with Shirley and I. On several occasions he got annoyed at us for no apparent reason. One day, he came to see us at Rogart, and his annoyance was bubbling over. He was demanding to know why I hated the Free Church. I advised him that as I ministered to people, the name above the door was not relevant as long as I could speak about Jesus, and Him crucified.

Despite all the negative things that happened in this period of time, we look back and say we were blessed. Rogart will always have fond memories and sad memories for us. It was there that Shirley's mother passed away on Christmas night in 2006. The love and kindness shown by the people (of all denominations and of none) astounded us, and we will always be grateful to them.

"PEOPLE WITH A MISSION" MINISTRIES

A group of Christian believers from Perth were mentioned in the previous chapter, and I would do them a dishonour to not mention them as part of our lives. They were like a well-drilled army unit under the leadership of pastors Mervyn and Jane Milne. Their military-styled Christian organisation had a vision from a prophetic utterance given many years ago to take God's power and presence back to the communities of Scotland. They were not disobedient to the Heavenly revelation by going into schools, doing street evangelism, having meetings for senior citizens and having outreach dinner meetings. But the ones we were most involved with were the extraordinary tent meetings up and down the nation and to the Islands of Scotland.

The people involved in the ministry were, and are, people sold out for the Gospel. Many souls have been and are being saved through this amazing work. I was privileged to have been chosen as the preacher at several of these tent meetings. To have witnessed souls saved and touched by the power of the Lord through this ministry has been such a blessing to Shirley and I. The tent meeting I remember the most clearly was in Dunvegan, on the Isle of Skye. I can still picture many young people walking up the centre aisle of the tent with tears streaming down their faces as they went forward to surrender their lives to Jesus.

I also remember a tent meeting in Newburgh, where I gained a following of young people who were evicted from the tent for their bad behaviour but congregated outside shouting, "Don-ald, Don-ald!" The gang leader was a young lady called Kadra, whom I will always remember for making me feel like a pop star!

CLAN MCLAUGHLAN

Over the years, we met and were influenced by some lovely people. For many years we had admired and loved the McLaughlan family. They were the first Pentecostal believers to set up a church in the Scottish Highlands. The late Paul and Sheila pastored the work of the Pentecostal Church of God in Lancashire before moving to the Scottish Highlands. They were led by the Holy Spirit to plant a church in Inverness. Supported by several of their family, they eventually purchased a church building in Friar Street, which has helped, supported, and blessed Christians and non-Christians for many, many years. Shirley and I were privileged to have known Paul and Sheila and to be inspired by their Christian walk.

On one occasion, Sheila was in prayer when the Holy Spirit told her to travel about twenty miles to the home of a lady she knew who was in grave danger. Being obedient to the Heavenly call, she jumped into the car and drove to this certain destination, finding the door of the property locked. She called the local police and asked them to break the door down, telling them that a young lady was in danger inside. They asked her who told her of this situation, to which she replied that it was the Holy Spirit. They looked at her and laughed, but this lady was adamant, and somehow she managed to persuade them to knock the door down. They discovered that this lady had cut her wrists in an effort to commit suicide and was very close to death. Calling on the medical profession, this lady's life was preserved. Sheila returned home with the joy of the Lord as a result of listening, hearing, and obeying the voice of her Saviour.

Stories like that were common to the McLaughlans. We drank in those challenging and encouraging testimonies every time we met. The church in Inverness is now pastored by their son Paul, with his wife Helen by his side. It continues to be blessed and be a blessing to many in the capital of the Scottish Highlands and further afield.

THE FISHERMAN'S HALL, BRORA

The Fisherman's Hall, Brora, was another oasis for us. It was a place where we were welcome. Ross and Margaret MacLeod were stalwarts in the community and church, always welcoming us with open arms. There were occasions when we stayed in the Free Church Manse, as there was no minister at the time.

On one of those occasions, we decided to organise a four-day mission in the Fisherman's Hall. A family came down from Orkney to be at these meetings. They had a motorhome and wanted to park outside the Manse, but we insisted that they use the house. We arranged a place for them to sleep, as the Manse was a big house with five or six bedrooms. This was Willie Buchan, his wife and twenty-two-year-old daughter, Jackie. His daughter had a curvature of her spine and was slightly disabled but very capable. She attended the meetings, but on the Sunday evening asked if I would be angry if she stayed at home. Assuring her that that was not a problem, I took her to the big living room and told her to watch television or whatever she wanted to do. She was surprised that I would allow her to watch television on a Sunday.

We all went to the meeting except Jackie, who was left warm and comfortable watching television. The meeting was very good, but nothing major happened. I was first home that night, and Jackie welcomed me, waving her arms frantically above her head. "What is wrong, Jackie?" I inquired. "Look! Look!" she said. "I can lift my hands above my head. I have been healed!" Not knowing of the restriction that this disability gave her, I was surprised to hear her say she had been healed.

She went on to tell me that since the age of fourteen, she had been unable to wash her own hair, but here she was with hands waving high above her head. Jackie's mother was the next person home, and Jackie was back in the hallway waving her hands above her head, once again, shouting, "Mum, look! Look, Mum!" Her mother knew right away what had happened and asked if I had prayed for her, to which I immediately answered that I had not. "Darling," she said to Jackie, "I think you have grown taller." Upon measuring Jackie's height, it was found that she had grown two inches (from four feet ten and a half inches to five feet and half an inch. That half-inch over five feet was very important to Jackie. It would appear that God had visited Jackie as she took time aside. Although she was not completely healed as we would have desired, doors opened for her to share her marvellous testimony.

Over the years, we had some amazing meetings in Brora's Fisherman's Hall. One evening, our friend from Canada, George MacKenzie, was with us, and the Holy Spirit invaded the building. After being prayed for, men and women were prostrate under the anointing power of the Holy Spirit. In the end, we had to prop some people against the wall as the Spirit of God touched them. Brora was precious to us.

At one time, a whole lot of young people came to the meetings and made professions of faith. However, there were many obstacles to their walk with the Lord. Some of those obstacles were churchy, religious Christians who wanted to bring condemnation and criticism, which caused many of those young boys and girls to walk away from God.

Shirley and I have a special love for the Scottish Highlands. It was as a young man working in the Royal Bank of Scotland that I first visited Lochinver. Later on, as Christians, we would take short weekend trips, which allowed me to reconnect with people I had not seen for a long time. Such a meeting was with Flora Matheson from Clachtoll, near Lochinver. I had been working locally in the Royal Bank of Scotland since I had left school, and the big, bright lights of the world outside of island life had not really interested me. I enjoyed playing football and had a good social life with many friends. It was normal procedure for the bank to transfer you to another branch after a few years, so that you could gain experience in different fields and cultures.

I was transferred to Lochinver on the North-West coast of Scotland. It was a small village with a thriving fishing industry. I settled into the community very quickly, and the social life was centred around the Culag Hotel (a well-known Highland Hotel where many famous and distinguished guests had stayed and enjoyed the solitude of the Highlands as well as the beautiful scenery).

FLORA MATHESON MEMORIES

It was here in Lochinver, as a wild young man, that I met Flora Matheson. I make specific mention of Flora for the following reasons. She worked with me in the bank around the middle of the seventies. She was a beautiful girl whom I dated for a short period of time. Many years later, after I had become a Christian, I revisited Lochinver. I met up with Flora, who had been through a broken marriage and lots of sadness since we had first met many years before. Her first husband had died, and she was in love with another man called Eck.

I told her about my faith in Jesus and that I was now a missionary and a preacher. She asked if I could officiate at weddings, to which I replied that I was a licensed pastor with International Gospel Outreach and that my license enabled me to marry people in any and various places. Sometime later, Flora called me to request that I officiate at her marriage to Eck at a fisherman's bothy on the coast at a village called Clachtoll, a few miles north of Lochinver. It was an amazing wedding. I recall that it was very windy. The great Atlantic Ocean was battering on the rocks a very short distance from the wee bothy, where Flora and Eck exchanged marriage vows.

Many years later, I got a call from a Free Church of Scotland minister. He had been requested to contact me and ask me to call and see Flora, who was in hospital in Inverness. She had cancer. Although the circumstances were not good, it was nice to see Flora again. She was poorly but positive, and at that time, the chemotherapy stayed the cancer for several years.

On a summer's evening, many years later, I got a call from Flora to say that she was back in hospital. She asked if it would be possible for me to see her in Inverness Royal Infirmary, where she was a patient. Flora was very practical, and my visit was really a final farewell. But it was Flora's eternal destiny and where she would spend it that was at stake here. She told me she had weeks to live and asked if I could officiate at her funeral. I explained that I was going to Eastern Europe for a few weeks, but I would be back, and delighted to fulfil her request. I then asked about her salvation. Her face lit up, and she responded this was the main reason she wanted to see me. She wanted to be saved, and asked if I could help her put her faith and trust in the Lord Jesus Christ.

In the quietness of her hospital ward, Flora gave her heart to Jesus and was saved. I left the hospital that day with a mixture of great sadness and great joy. We were back some weeks later, and Flora was my immediate priority. I phoned her daughter to be told that she was home at Clachtoll and that she was peaceful but passing away. It was late on a Saturday night, and we stayed at Shirley's brother's house in Golspie, in the Scottish Highlands. The following morning, we made our way west to Clachtoll when we received a phone call that Flora had died.

A few days later, at an old church in a neighbouring village, hundreds crammed in to say a final farewell to Flora. I could testify on her behalf about that day in the hospital some weeks earlier when she had surrendered her life to the Lordship of Jesus Christ. On the back of that statement, I could preach of the only One Who can truly bring salvation to a lost soul. I preached Jesus, just as Phillip preached Jesus down in Samaria two thousand years before me.

With this, I brought some humour when I said that Flora had been my girlfriend many years previously and had dumped me for a better man. The Gospel message was clear, and you could feel a heavy anointing over the meeting. The silence was deafening as I spoke of the beautiful Saviour. The presence of the Lord was tangible.

Later, in the cemetery, a hush of solemnity and awe came over those who attended. The undertaker was lost for words. He could see that the people had no desire to go home, and he wanted to finalise his work at the grave. A lovely elderly man (whom I later learned was a Presbyterian church elder) came over to me and explained in a strong west-coast accent how concerned he was at the joyful stories I had told in the church. He continued that he had never been at a funeral like it in his life, and that the sense of God's presence was so mighty (something he had not witnessed for many, many years). He said that he had never heard the Gospel preached in such a simple way, and his facial expression broke into a smile. To help the undertaker, I closed this solemn time in prayer to the background sound of the Atlantic Ocean lapping on a nearby shore. Later, at the hotel where we went to have teas and coffees, many inquired about the salvation that Flora had experienced We were pleased to direct them to Jesus and the cross and for them to look to Him for salvation, which is great and free.

HEADING NORTH TO ORKNEY

Being invited by Willie Buchan to do a mission in Orkney, we were blessed by the reception we received from various church leaders. After several days of visiting other islands (to get a sense of how and what to pray about), we rented the Boy Scouts' Hall for a week of mission. During these tours, we went to Eday, where again, we were welcomed by some lovely and amazing people.

We stayed with Maris and her husband John and slept in a horsehair bed in a room where the Atlantic Ocean came into the bedroom (if the tide was high and a strong westerly wind blew). Both Maris and John would have been retired but had come away from the "rat race." They loved their new life on the island of Eday, which had a population of one hundred and forty-four people. As I write this, I can almost smell the bread that Maris baked every morning.

During meetings on Eday, we led seven people to the Lord, and we used to say that five per cent of the population got saved! We also met a man who was a well-known pop star in his day, and he led the worship on keyboards at several house meetings we were at.

MISSION IN KIRKWALL

Back on the main island of Orkney, souls were being saved, and we were so busy that we needed help. We sent for John Purcell to come and help us. David Robinson also came. It was decided by the church leader to erect a tent, as it would attract more people. The tent was erected, and although we worked out of the hall during the day, it was tent meetings in the evenings.

It was June, but a cold north wind decided to visit us. The meetings were very much influenced by the cold weather, but we stuck to the plan like good missionaries. Over the week, we helped several people come to know the salvation of the Lord. However, if I may pick "the cream of the crop," it was on the last evening. A lady walked in wearing a "Rab C Nesbitt string vest" and very little else above the waistline. She had come from the small island of Eday.

Her first words to me were, "I'm a pagan. Am I welcome here?" I assured her she was if she had come for the right reasons (and that right reason was to hear the gospel). John Purcell preached that evening, and she sat on the front row. Being dubious of her intention, I sat near her in case she attacked the preacher. As John continued in his firebrand style, she began to perspire, although the temperature in the hall was moderate. She then became agitated. As John made the invitation for souls to come forward for prayer, she was the first person up, desiring to repent and come to the Lord and be saved.

Later, she told us that as a young girl, she had trusted Jesus and had been baptised as a believer, but years later, she got caught up in witchcraft. That night, she was restored and delivered. A few days later, she invited everyone on the island of Eday to come to see her burn her witchcraft books and other occultic paraphernalia.

Another strange event happened in Orkney during our mission there. I told a funny story about Wing Wong and Sing Song. It is about a young Chinese couple who met playing ping pong. They fell in love, married, and built a wee house down by the river. Wing Wong, the man of the house, was expected to collect water from the river every morning. With the water, Sing Song did the washing, cooking, cleaning, baking and so on. He had two buckets made of clay to collect the water, and everything was going well.

Every day when he came back from the river, she would say, "親愛的，你是女人想要的最棒的丈夫。 我愛你." That means: "Darling, you are the most wonderful husband a woman could want. I love you."

This continued for a while, but one day he cracked a bucket. That day, there were no terms of endearment. All she said was: "你這個愚蠢的愚蠢的人，你已經破解了桶." That means: "You stupid, stupid person. You have cracked the bucket."

Every day, as he returned, there was one full bucket and one half-empty bucket. This really annoyed Sing Song, and she would express her anger.

She would say:

"你能不能修好這個愚蠢的水桶你這個愚蠢的人." That means: "Can you not fix the stupid bucket? You stupid man."

Many months later, he asked her to walk with him down to the river. On one side of the path were the most beautiful flowers. "Why did you not grow them on both sides?" she inquired in Chinese. "I did," he said, "but they only grew on the side where the cracked pot watered them every morning."

The moral of the story is that God will use cracked pots. So, I said that if you are a cracked pot here tonight, God can use you. Now, you must understand that I was pretending to speak Chinese as I told that story. In the congregation that evening, there was a Chinese couple. He was a Professor of Agriculture at the UHI (the University of the Highlands and Islands in Orkney.)

He approached me afterwards and said, "Pastor Donald, you speak very good Mandarin. I speak Cantonese, but I understood everything you said! In my shock and surprise, I did not have the heart to ask him what I had said, but he appeared very happy! *But God…"*

BILLY AND IRENE

We made several trips to Orkney and, on one occasion, were accompanied by our friends, Rob and Pat Kiff. Rob was a retired professor of marine biology, and had pastored a church in Manchester. Upon returning to mainland Scotland, we were asked to call and see Billy and Irene in Thurso, as Billy had cancer and wanted prayer to be made for his healing. The welcome was warm and friendly, and Irene had Scotch pies ready for us. As we enjoyed our tea, Irene began to tell us how she had a spirit and the power of a spirit.

She told us that, on occasions, she would stand at the window and watch a man coming up the road on a bicycle. She did not like this certain gentleman and would shout, "Fall! Fall!" and he would fall. She had approached the local minister to organise a spiritualist church, but they were unwilling. "I like people who have the spirit," she went on. Mr. and Mrs. Kiff were at this time changing colours and wanted to leave, but I was in no big hurry to leave as Irene was warming up another Scotch pie for me.

When the Scotch pie was safely delivered onto my plate, I gently said to Irene that she was channelling into the wrong side of the spirit realm. I said that we, as born-again Christians, were of the Holy Spirit, but the spirits in operation through her were from the dark side. I will always remember her response: "Don't tell me that, Donald. Do you mean I am not on Jesus' side?" Gently assuring her that this was the prognosis of us all, she asked: "What must I do?" We were able to point her to Jesus. She renounced her occultic practices, and the joy that filled her soul was visible for all to see. "Billy, what about you?" she asked her man. "Oh, I would love to have Jesus in my heart, Irene," he said. So we led Billy to Christ. We also prayed with Billy about his cancer and left shortly afterwards. It was a full and fulfilling day's work.

Sometime later, Billy and Irene moved across the water to live in Orkney. We visited them one Saturday morning, with Willie Buchan and John Purcell accompanying us. They were delighted to see us and welcomed us in. They were both assured of their salvation, and we rejoiced with them, but Irene said, "I have something to tell you, Donald." A fear of her telling me she was back into that "spiritual mode" came over me, but that was not the case. "Something is troubling me," she said. "Since the day Billy and I gave our hearts to the Lord, it has troubled us." We inquired about the situation, and she told us that although she and Billy had been co-habiting for over thirty years, they were never married in the eyes of God. "Yes," she said, "in the eyes of the law, we are common-law married, but I want to put that right if possible. I want to be married in the eyes of God. I do not want to go to a church or make a big thing of it, as people think we are properly married, even our own family."

As quick as lightning, Shirley was on her feet. "You can marry them, Donald," she said. "Yes, Donald's got a license to marry you, Irene. He can do it right now." It is a known fact that Shirley can get me into a lot of trouble! I explained to Billy and Irene that they could make promises before God and enter into a marriage covenant as long as they did not want the paperwork, as this would take time. There would have to be the marriage banns and all the other stuff attached to a marriage ceremony. They both agreed that this was "a God thing," as being common-law husband and wife, they had no need for paperwork.

Shirley and Irene disappeared into the bedroom, from which Irene returned with a beautiful kaftan. Billy was wearing a white tee shirt. I was leading them through the words of the marriage ceremony, right up to the phrase: "I now pronounce you man and wife. You may now kiss the bride." It was a serious, though funny moment, but you felt that God was uniting them in a way only God can.

A few years later, we heard that Billy had died, and being in the North of Scotland, we went over to Orkney to see Irene. Irene was well. She was missing Billy but still going on with Jesus. As we left, these were her words to us: "Donald and Shirley Buchanan, you have been with me on two of the happiest days of my life. The day I gave my heart to Jesus, and the day I married Billy." Hallelujah. *"But God…"*

YOUTH MISSIONS

Another exciting annual event in our diary was taking young people on mission. We recall going to Portugal and going into the street, giving out Gospel tracts and invitations to evening meetings. During the meetings, we would share testimonies and sing, and I would preach.

At the end of one such meeting, I did the normal altar call for people wanting to seek for salvation. A gentleman of Black/African/American descent responded to the call for salvation. His eyes were very bloodshot, and his teeth were crooked and broken. As I prayed with him, others translated the prayer into Portuguese. He was repenting of his sin and accepting Christ as his Saviour. Soon, he grew very angry and agitated. We had to hold his arms, but as he was fighting against us, we recognised something demonic manifesting. As we wrestled him to the ground, we continued to pray over him until peace reigned and there was a release from the bondage of the spirits which controlled him.

The next day, I was in the hall on my own, when this same man came in. He was excited and came over to me, lifting me up and down like a rag doll, shouting something in Portuguese that I did not understand. Hearing the commotion, others came in from the kitchen area as the man was over-excited. They translated what he was saying as: "I slept! I slept!" This man had been a mercenary soldier in Angola during a civil war there. Angola was a former Portuguese colony. He had killed men, women and children, and every night when he closed his eyes, flashbacks came to him, and he couldn't sleep.

In accepting Jesus as Saviour and Lord, peace came to his heart and he slept. In his acceptance of Jesus, he had been born again and completely set free from the demonic strongholds of his life. Jesus had set him free. Hallelujah.

Mission with the young ones was always a fun time. I used to say it was the most stressful two weeks of the year, but yet the most enjoyable. One year, we were in Killarney in the South of Ireland. Again, the programme was to give out tracts, sing and share testimonies in the street. Some of the young men and women would dance to Christian music and songs. The dances were usually choreographed by themselves and were a wonderful means of bringing a crowd to gather in the town centres. We would then share a quick testimony, and the crowd would change, and so on. Sometimes you had to make space for yourselves, and one year I remember paying a busker ten euros to go for a cup of tea whilst I took his pitch to share the Gospel! It was reported that I had bribed him, but at times, things need to happen for the greater good.

Another time, I stood on a plinth in Tralee, and as I shared the Gospel, many came to take photos. It was a small marketplace with stalls (some selling IRA paraphernalia and CDs of Irish Rebel songs). Intrigued by the attention I was being given, I looked around, and there on the wall behind me was a big mural of Bobby Sands. Bobby Sands was one of the men who starved themselves to death during the "Troubles" in Ireland. This man's mural and not me was the centre of attention, and it was what attracted the photographers. I still managed to preach the Word of God, but no one responded that day.

A favourite place for us to do our outreach was in front of St Mark's church in Portadown. We had made many friends over the years in that area, but again, one situation stands out above the rest.

The young girls were dancing, and an elderly lady stood aside, watching and listening to the Christian songs, the testimonies, and the preaching. I remember approaching her, sensing a loneliness and a longing within her. She was well in her seventies (maybe more), and I asked if she was enjoying the outreach. "Oh, very much," she said. I asked, "Are you a Christian lady yourself?" "Oh", she said, "I am not, and I wish I was." She told me that since the age of twelve she had wanted to be saved, but no one ever told her how she could be saved. After a few more minutes of conversation, Shirley and a young man called John were leading her to Jesus. What I remember the most about that day was when she skipped across the paving slabs, telling people she had been saved, as she went to catch a bus to Enniskillen.

During those days on mission, our favourite place to stay was at John and Doreen Greenaway's River of Life Centre. We wanted the young people to experience the Holy Spirit for themselves. I remember one evening at a meeting, the anointing was so heavy upon John, that as the young ones went to be prayed for, the power of God which came through John not only knocked them to the ground, but physically threw them to the floor in a wonderful display of God's power. It was like touching twenty-two thousand volts of electricity!

John and a few others were always keen to pray for the young ones. One night, however, I insisted that the young ones should be given the opportunity to pray for others. One pastor, called Adrian, wishing to encourage the young ones, came forward, and two young ladies lifted their hands to pray for impartation for him. To our surprise, the Holy Spirit sent power through them that hit this lovely man, and he was flat out on the floor under the anointing of the Holy Spirit for several minutes. Another evening, as the young ones waited upon the Lord, they gathered in a circle. As their young hearts desired more of God, one after another was touched by the invisible hand of the Master, and each one went out in the power of the Spirit. It was wonderful to behold. It was gentle, peaceful, simple; it was God at work, filling those dear young ones with more of His power.

THE EVIE REID STORY

Whilst back in the North of Scotland, we visited Brora again. It was our favourite wee town in Scotland. Brora Fisherman's Hall was where we first met Evie Reid during a mission. We used the hall as a place to serve teas and coffees as a means of meeting people. Evie walked in. She had hair like an Afro hairstyle, and her appearance was what can best be described as dishevelled. Evie was 48 years old. She had done drugs, alcohol, and men. She had two children, Kevin, aged 27, and Mhairi, aged 11. They both suffered challenges from health issues, as did Evie.

Evie was depressed and often attended clinics for help. She walked with her head hung low, looking at her feet as she walked. There was a sense of guilt and shame in her demeanour. Her attendance at school as a child was not good, and she could not read or write very well. We warmly welcomed her into the hall, asking her if she wanted tea or coffee. "I don't suppose your Jesus would take me," she said. I replied that the hymn-writer (Fanny Crosby) put it this way: "The vilest offender who truly believes, that moment from Jesus a pardon receives." I explained that the Scriptures would support that statement, but as Evie had either been drinking or doing drugs that day, I did not want to encourage her to pray a salvation prayer, as I could not be sure if she was a genuine seeker of Christ.

We asked her to call again the next day if she was serious about coming to Jesus in repentance. To our shock, who walked in the next day? It was Evie. She had cleaned herself up, her hair was brushed, and she now looked a lot better than she was the day before. As we sat and talked, she told us that as a young child, she had given her heart to Jesus, but time and trials had destroyed her life. She had guilt, shame, regrets, and remorse, and soon she was in a state of brokenness, repenting and asking Jesus for forgiveness. As mercy and grace poured over her, Evie was delivered from her sin.

The next day, the local minister's wife noticed that something had happened to Evie because her head was lifted high, and the shame, guilt and condemnation had now gone in Jesus' name. Some weeks later, she was baptised by total immersion in the local swimming pool in Brora and was not afraid to speak and share her newfound faith in Jesus Christ. It was wintertime. In March of the following year, we were in Killarney ministering, when the phone rang. It was Helen, Evie's sister, telling us that Evie had died. She had a heart disease; whether she was aware of it or not, we do not know. She died in the bath and was found by her daughter Mhairi, who woke Kevin. It was three o'clock in the morning.

The situation in that house must have been awful, but Kevin, being big and strong, lifted her out of the bath and called Helen, who organised everything else. Helen asked us if we were able to come back for the funeral, as the local minister wanted us to give testimony of our knowledge of Evie's salvation. We drove from Killarney to Brora, and the following day, we were ready for the funeral. I gave the eulogy and spoke of our assurance that Evie was safely in the arms of Jesus. On the next page is a letter we found in Evie's cupboard some time after the funeral, as we helped tidy up the house and prepare Evie's stuff for the local charity shop.

The latter has been described as a 'masterpiece.' I have made over ten thousand Gospel tracts using Evie's 'masterpiece,' and they have found their way to various places worldwide. One doctor in the South of England saw it and wanted five hundred to place in his surgery, telling us that he would give one to every person suffering depression who would be a patient at his surgery.

Another situation arose on the day of Evie's funeral. We learned that Mhairi's father had come to take her back to stay with him. He was a known alcoholic, and Helen was concerned that should Mhairi go to live with him, she would be an alcoholic in a short space of time. She had promised Evie that should anything happen to her, she would look after Mhairi and Kevin, although Kevin was fit enough to look after himself. We devised a plan to "kidnap" Mhairi and take her back to Ireland with us, as we were speaking at a conference near Dungannon, in Northern Ireland, a few days later. Helen would approach the Social Services to foster Mhairi and then come to Ireland to take her back home.

When the church service was over, Shirley and Mhairi would slip out a side door and head for Inverness, which was sixty miles away. I would join them later, get a ferry back to Ireland, and Mhairi would be safe. At the graveside, Kevin came over and asked where his sister was. I tried to explain that, with Helen's permission, we had taken her for safekeeping, to Ireland. Kevin weighed over thirty stones at that time. He smoked and used illegal drugs. He refused to understand that we were doing this with good intentions. He was not willing that we would take Mhairi without him, as he now saw himself as Mhairi's caretaker.

You can read Evie's letter on the next page.

TO NIGHT I WANT TO SHARE
WITH YOU WHAT THE LORD
JEASUS HAS DON FOR ME
HE HAS GAVE ME SOW MUTCH
PEASE IN MY HART AND JOY
HE HAS DON A LOT FOR
ME IN THIS WE WHILE
SINCE I CAME A CHRISTAN
IF SOME PEAPLE ARNT
CHRISTANS PLEAS GIVE
YOUR HARTS TO HIM
 IF NOT YOU WILL NEVER
HAVE PEACE OR JOY ONLE
TERMENT WITH THE
DEVIL AND BE IN A BIG
DARK HOLE WITH JESUS
YOU WILL ALWAS BE
 IN THE LIGHT.
I ALWAS THOT I WAS NOTHING
BUT NOW AM NOT NOTHING
I HAVE JEASUS

THE KEVIN REID STORY

Kevin told me he was coming to Ireland to look after Mhairi, as he was going to be her guardian. When I objected to him coming (explaining that we were going to stay at a Christian Centre and he would not fit in), he threatened to get the police, as we had kidnapped Mhairi. The reality of his statement was that this was indeed the case, good as the intentions were. Knowing how difficult this could get, I agreed, on the condition that he did not drink or do drugs if he stayed at this Centre.

A few nights later, we were at the meeting at the River of Life, with Pastor John Greenaway. I was the preacher, and at the end of my sermon, I encouraged people who were convicted of their sin to come forward and surrender their lives to Jesus, and for others to come and be healed or be Baptised in the Holy Ghost. A young person approached me and said that their Scottish friend was crying. It was Kevin. I immediately assumed that he had come out of the cloud of stupor that drugs had given him to the realisation that his mum had died, and I went to console him. "Have you realised your mum has died, Kevin?" I asked. "Of course I have," he grunted. So I asked what the tears were for, and he replied that he wanted to go to the front and give his heart to Jesus.

This man never went to church (possibly a few funerals) and never knew about salvation, redemption, justification, or whatever. From a natural standpoint his desire may have seemed out of place, as his theology would not have been in order. He simply wanted to go to the front and give his heart to Jesus. I could not refuse such a request. As I led him in a sinner's prayer, I felt that this was stupidity and that this was not Christianity or reality. He could not be understanding the need for the conviction of sin or repentance.

After I finished praying a prayer of salvation with him (with Doreen Greenaway beside me), we asked if we could pray for him to be Baptised in the Spirit. As we prayed, the Holy Spirit touched him. Thirty-plus stones of weight hit the floor, and the whole building shook. It was a portacabin, so the effects of Kevin hitting the floor caused vibration throughout the whole building. Kevin was out in the Spirit, and shortly afterwards, someone came over and said that he was speaking in tongues. Bending down beside him, I could clearly hear this gift which many would seek, in operation. Kevin went home to Brora a few days later, and the following Saturday, he was out beside the local Co-op shop, distributing Gospel tracts. He was a young man who had been transformed. As far as we know, he has never smoked cigarettes since. As far as we know, he has never drunk alcohol since that time. He has never done drugs since that moment. Kevin can still testify of his salvation, going back to that amazing night at the River of Life Healing Centre and church. *"But God…"*

RATHKEALE, IRELAND

It was Tom Maguire who took me to the South of Ireland to meet Christian believers. We stopped at a town called Rathkeale, just south of Limerick. This town was predominantly a Travellers' town. That particular weekend, it was busier than usual, as there was to be a wedding, and many Travellers had come over from Tottenham, in London, for the special occasion. Tom took me to meet one of his friends, and in the house, he introduced me as a pastor from Scotland. I was asked to pray for a lady who was visiting. When she left the house, she went and told others that a man was praying for the sick in her friend's home. Soon, there was a queue of people asking for prayer. With God's favour clearly upon my life that day, we were seeing people healed and blessed, and we believe many came to faith in Christ. After some time, the queue abated, and I needed to meet up with Tom.

As I walked up the street, a large 4 x 4 vehicle pulled up beside me. Out jumped this pretty young lady and asked if I was the 'holy man!' Looking around and seeing no one else in the vicinity, I stammered that I must be. She lifted three small children out of the vehicle and asked if I would pray a blessing on them. There, in the middle of the street of a town of some four thousand people, on what was already an extraordinary day, I was laying hands on those lovely children, and asking the Lord to bless them. I came across a caravan site further down the street. I had some Gospel tracts to distribute and went from caravan to caravan giving them out.

I was getting a good reception for my efforts to share the Gospel and having some lovely and interesting conversations about the Lord Jesus Christ as I told people of God's love for them. Many Travellers do have a faith in Christ, but they have a lot of superstition mixed in with that faith. I knocked on the door of one of the caravans and was met by a lovely lady who told me that she was a very religious woman. I advised her that I was not a religious man, as it was religious people who had crucified Jesus. I explained to her that the Jews were religious people, and that their religion had blinded them to the Man Who came to redeem them and save their souls. This lady was adamant about what she believed and showed me her statues of St Martin de Porres. She opened another cupboard, and there was a statue of St Thomas. Another had St Joseph, and upon informing her that I was "a Jesus man," she quickly opened another cupboard and said, "I have him too!"

Late in the day, I met a lady called Catherine. She told me about her husband, J.J., and how he was troubled with nightmares. She asked if I could pray for him. He would possibly not be home until midnight. The gypsy encampment was alive with music and laughter, and a good number were enjoying a drink or two. I was having a great time witnessing to these lovely people about Jesus as the hours passed by.

I went to Catherine and J.J.'s caravan. It was well after midnight. Catherine was waiting for J.J. to come home. She adamantly told me she did not believe in this "Jesus, Mary, and Joseph stuff" and that she went straight to God. I asked how she managed that, as the Scriptures clearly say, that Jesus said, "I am the way, the truth and the life: no man comes to the Father, but by Me. (John 14:6). I then quoted 1 Timothy 2:5, which tells us that there is one mediator between God and men, the Man, Christ Jesus. I also told her the Bible said that there is no other name under Heaven, whereby we must be saved (Acts 4:12). A pregnant pause entered our conversation, after which Catherine said, "I never saw that before. I never knew that before." As I watched, I saw this lady get born again before my very eyes. The revelation of God's wonderful Word had quickened her spirit to believe and receive, and be wonderfully transformed from darkness to light. It was like seeing a rose blossoming before my eyes.

After this, for some unknown reason, she prayed that well-known sinner's prayer. But I do not believe it was necessary, as the gracious salvation of the Lord had transformed this lovely lady and taken her from the grip of Satan's lies, saving her to the uttermost.

J.J. came back, and upon entering the caravan, Catherine had him by the lapels! "Listen to this man," she said. "Listen to him." I explained the way of salvation to J.J., but a few different spirits were fighting for his soul that night. Although he prayed a prayer accepting Jesus as his Saviour, I could not be completely sure as to how genuine he was. He prayed a prayer, possibly sincerely and genuinely, but Catherine had had an encounter with God.

I finally met up with Tom. It was almost three o'clock in the morning. Someone had promised us a place to stay, but having been taken up with all the excitement, we forgot to get back in time, and they had gone to bed, locking their door. We went to a local hotel where a night porter was on duty and paid an extortionate price for a room, even though it was after three o'clock in the morning.

The next morning, we went round to see J.J. and Catherine, introducing them to Tom. Without us knowing it, J.J. and Catherine had come over from Tottenham, North London, for their daughter's wedding which was that day. Catherine had them all primed by her witness of Jesus, and as we arrived, they were all outside the caravan, lined up, maybe awaiting a photographer or someone like that. Catherine had shared the Gospel with them all, and now she said, "Here is the man who will pray with you to accept Christ as your Saviour." There was the bride-to-be, the bridesmaids and the flower girls. It was something you could dream about but never see. Here were these lovely young ladies praying for forgiveness and mercy from the Lord God Almighty, in Jesus' name, praying to be saved, in a little gypsy town called Rathkeale.

MARY KING MEMORIES

Over the following years, Shirley and I made many visits to the South of Ireland, to Killarney, Tralee, Abbeyfeale and other towns and villages. An amazing woman called Mary King lived in Abbeyfeale. She wanted us to stay with her when we were there and treated us like royalty, although Mary was a widow.

At the time, Desi, her son, was going through trials with depression, suffering quite badly at times from real moments of darkness. Can I immediately say that through other people's ministry and God's goodness, Desi is now completely healed and out evangelising and preaching the Gospel. Mary did not have an immersion heater or central heating in her home. Without us knowing, she was up at the crack of dawn every day to have the fires lit so that the water would be heated and the place would be warm when we got up. She had an amazing servant's heart and was such a blessing to us. Sadly, Mary passed away in June 2023, but I am sure that a glorious welcome was made for her in Heaven.

TEACHING IN A CATHOLIC CHURCH

One night, we were invited to speak at Saint John's Catholic church in Tralee. I was asked to talk about the Holy Spirit. On the day I was due to speak, the Holy Spirit would not allow me to talk about the Holy Spirit. Without a subject, title or note on paper, Shirley and I met up with a lady called Grace, who had invited us. I believe we were meant to speak to the charismatic wing of the church.

I went without plans, open to the Lord's leading. Grace wanted us to see the garden, and we felt she was stalling us for some reason. I am the type of man who would rather look at concrete than look at flowers! It was cold outside, so we encouraged Grace to take us inside. When inside, we were in the midst of a "praying the rosary" meeting. Although I was relaxed enough about it, Shirley was very unsettled, saying, "I'm not staying here," and, "I'm leaving." But I managed to settle her, and when a couple of priests went away with a few others, we were left with our congregation for the evening.

Introductions having been made, I stood up with a Bible in my hand, and out of my mouth began to come words letting them know of my admiration of their zeal for prayer and their adoration of the Virgin Mary. I then said that having been brought up Catholic, I now knew that they were in error, which was so wrong and not in line with Scripture. Seeing the end of my life coming before me, I continued to say that repetitive prayers were not the kind of prayers Jesus wanted but prayers from the heart. I continued to say that praying to Mary was unacceptable to God, as the only prayers He accepted were those made through the name of His dear and precious Son, Jesus. Such council was not only enough to kill me, but enough to bury me (whether with or without a mass, I was not sure)! Shirley was (by this time a strange colour of white) suggesting I sit down, but the man still had a sermon to preach with the full permission of the Holy Spirit.

At the end, questions were asked about Purgatory. I confidently told them that such teaching was not found in the Scriptures. Two souls wanted to be saved, and the janitor of the building wanted us all out as soon as possible, but some people wanted prayer. A man called Christopher asked about his Catholic medallions hanging around his neck. I told him they were like idols, which God called an abomination. I said that they were like a god to him, believing that such a thing as a dead piece of metal could change or influence things in his life. The night ended, and we were never asked back. But I believe we will be remembered.

ETIL AND HER SON, MARCUS

We met so many wonderful people on our visits to the South of Ireland. There are far too many to give a mention of them all. One person springs to mind, however: a beautiful lady called Ethel (in her own accent, she would say "Etil"). She got saved ("born again") through a health service course to help her get over depression. She baptised herself in the bath and was going on with God. She had one son called Marcus. Marcus lived in Cork City and was not a believer. He had a well-paid, important job and often visited his mother in Killarney.

One evening, we had been invited to a meal at "Etil's" house, and Marcus was visiting her. He was a tall, good-looking, young man, but he was not pleased with us from the moment he set eyes on us. "Who are you?" he inquired, "and what are you doing here?" His mother was in the kitchen finalising our dinner. "I don't like you," he said. "You make me sick. Even looking at you makes me sick."

We apologized profusely and were willing to leave. However, Marcus left the room, only to come back a few minutes later to confirm that I was unsettling his life. He left the room for the second time, returning with a teeshirt which had some Chinese or Japanese writing on it. "What do you make of this?" he said. "I make nothing of it," I said. "I do not know what that writing says, so I would not wear it." "Keep it," he said. "Keep it, throw it away, or burn it."

A few minutes later, we heard him being violently sick in the toilet. He came back in again with another couple of items for me to take or burn. He did not join us at the table for the meal, but I believe he was glad when our time came to leave. Several days later, we learned that Marcus had been wonderfully saved, and had a powerful gift of the discerning of spirits.

Sometime later, he got married, and the last we heard of him, he was working in Edinburgh and had a small family. It would appear that the Spirit in us was affecting the comfort of the spirit in him, and when he was delivered from that spirit (as he was sick), the Holy Spirit moved in to save him. It could possibly (and probably) have been due to his mother's prayers.

MY FRIEND, JOHN ALICK

My best friend in secondary school and later teenage years, was a man called John Alick. It would be wise not to tell any stories about our exploits, but I can say we had some exciting times together. Once, when Shirley and I were in Killarney, I got a phone call from my brother Allan telling me that John Alick was very ill with cancer and may not have long to live.

The relationship between John Alick and I had become strained as a result of my leaving the Catholic church. But here I was, travelling to various places to preach and teach the Holy Scriptures, believing the Holy Bible was the truth, and pointing to Jesus to find eternal life (John 14). I was not sure where John Alick was with God. I believed I needed to go and share God's Word with him, and we drove from Killarney to Larne, crossed over to Cairnryan, and then up to the Hebrides. It was a journey of six hundred and fifty miles, plus four and a half hours on the two ferries. It was a full day's journey. Upon arrival, I phoned Annabel, his wife. It was a Sunday, and we planned to leave on Monday, as we had appointments to fulfil.

She told me that her dear husband was too tired to see Shirley and I, as there had been many visitors that day. She asked if we could call the next evening as she believed he would be in bed until late afternoon. We told her of our predicament, and being protective of her husband's well-being, she said there was little she could do. The next day, we deliberately drove through the village of Torlum early in the morning, in order to pass John Alick's house.

Driving slowly past his house, we thought we saw John Alick's silhouette through the windows. Calling at his house on the off-chance, we were welcomed by Annabel and John Alick. This lovely, dear man was never overweight; however, now he was but a shadow of himself. I told him the very reason we called. I told him that we wanted to pray for him. We brought some Gospel tracts for him to read (a tract is a small leaflet which gives a short Gospel message and points us to Christ). As I spoke, he was already reading the tracts and asked if he could pray what we call a sinner's prayer.

A sinner's prayer is something like this: *"Dear Lord Jesus, I am a sinner. I believe You died for sinners, and therefore You died for me. I am asking for Your mercy and forgiveness, and want You to come into my heart and be my Lord and Saviour."* When believing this prayer by faith, as that faith meets the grace of God, new life comes to anyone who sincerely prays it.

That day, John Alick prayed that prayer carefully and sincerely, and I then prayed for his healing. I will always remember John Alick's words as he said, "It is a win-win situation I have, isn't it? If I die, I will go to be with Jesus. If I get healed, I will be able to stay with Annabel for another while." It was a wonderful moment and a confession of faith.

SOME FUNNY MOMENTS

Over the years, we visited Benbecula many times, calling to see family and friends. But we write with regret that the Fellowship we started many years previously has come to an end. The Nursery School where we met and in which we had some awesome meetings had been destroyed in a strong Hebridean gale-force wind. Most of the islanders were either Catholics, or Protestants, or non-believers in God.

When we stayed there, one of our friends was Dolly Cameron. Dolly was well in her eighties and a Free Presbyterian. She could be a little more legal and stricter in her beliefs than we were. We identified as Pentecostals, believing the whole counsel of God's Word. We believed Jesus to be the same yesterday, today and forever (Hebrews 13:8), but that did not stop us from loving one another. Dolly always insisted on being helpful and always wanted to do our washing or help in any way she possibly could. It was always a joy to visit Dolly.

On one occasion, Shirley gave Dolly some washing to satisfy her longing to be helpful. Dolly was given my underwear and socks, even though most of them were clean. Being from the old school, Dolly would not use detergents and washing powder but boiled every item until every germ was surrendering its position and any rights it had to be on our clothes. The washing was dried, ironed, and presented to Shirley. All were folded, and placed back in the suitcase.

Some nights later, I was preaching at a meeting. As Pentecostals, we sometimes have experiences in the Holy Ghost, and these experiences can vary. One such experience is that we can shake or tremble under the anointing. As I preached that evening, I felt my underwear heading downwards towards my knees! Without a second thought, I took control of them from the outside of my trousers. It was then the turn of my socks to try and hide in my shoes, but I rescued them!

This went on many times throughout the meeting, as I began to conclude that Dolly's boiling of my clothes had been disastrous to the elastic in the socks and underwear. However, I managed to keep my composure and dignity and finished my sermon. As I met the congregation later, they all felt I had been under some kind of special anointing as I preached because of the jerking and movements I had been making. The congregation responded to what they believed was the power of God in operation! I did not reveal that the secret to an exciting evening was Dolly and the boiling pot destroying the elastic in my underwear and socks!

Many funny things can happen in Christian Ministry. We often pray for people and, at times, anoint them with oil for healing (James 5:14). I usually carry a small bottle of oil in my pocket, but on one occasion, as I smelled the oil, it was a little rancid and did not smell too good. It was Christmas time, so I added some cinnamon fragrance to the oil, making it smell nice. As I prayed for a certain lady, I put the oil on my thumb, placed my thumb on her forehead, and prayed. She was quick to tell me that she sensed a wonderful heat going through her forehead, and believed God had touched and healed her. I applied a little of the oil to the back of my hand, and indeed, the concoction was potent, leaving my skin with a burning sensation and a circular red mark visible for days!

I met this lady a few days later, and she, too, had a round red mark on her forehead. She was "over the moon," explaining to me that the healing touch of the Lord had been visible for all to see, and the mark had been a witness to her healing. She was able to testify to many about the mark God had left on her forehead as He had healed her. She was so excited and healed that I did not have the gumption to tell her that the oil should have carried a toxic warning! But her belief brought her to accept the prayer of faith, and she was marvellously healed.

A VISIT TO KENYA

Somewhere along the journey of life, we got invited to Kenya with Gilbert and Margaret Edgerton. We took our friend, Sandy Rogart, with us, and when we arrived, we stayed in a hostel-type place for the first night. There was a double bed in one room and a bunk bed in the other, all made ready for us. At times, Shirley has brainstorms, and wanted Sandy to sleep in the double bed while we would use the bunk beds, insisting that this was a better plan, despite my objection.

The evening came to an end, and it was bedtime. I went to the toilet at the end of a corridor, and upon my return, Shirley was lying in the lower bunk, having convinced Sandy that her plan was the better one. As I looked at the bed, the top bunk was about six feet off the ground, with no ladder to be found. Having an option to practise the Fosbury flop (a high jump technique) or another means of getting into bed, I decided that a run at the bed was the only alternative. With a run and a jump, I managed to get up so far, with my arms keeping me up and my legs dangling over Shirley's bed. I was wearing my shirt and underwear, and Shirley, laughing, said, "You look like Kermit the Frog!"

The picture of that moment still haunts me to this day. It was one of those moments that was just not funny, although Shirley still laughs at the remembrance of it. Eventually, I made it to bed, but the fear of falling out of it at this great height did not allow me much sleep that night.

The next day, it was off to the orphanage, where we were planning to work. Sandy was a great worker, able to put his hand to every work conceivable, whether painting, joinery, bricklaying, or whatever. I was also good at DIY. The staple diet was ugali, which is like porridge and wallpaper paste mixed together! When you put it in your mouth, it stuck there, not allowing you to swallow or remove it from your mouth by spitting it out. After a few days, I decided I could live on a diet of bananas and Coca-Cola!

Outside the grounds of the orphanage, there was a very small shop which sold my requirements. The light in the shanty wee building was from a letter-box type window at the front, which you spoke through. The lady in the shop ran a good business, as one day, she sold me a small, half-full container of sweeteners for something like eight pounds. But her real profit was not made by what she sold, but by a very sad story which she told.

"How are you today?" I said, in my efforts to begin a conversation. "Oh, very sad," was the reply. "Very, very sad. My mother lived far away - far, far away - and she has died, and I cannot get to the funeral." She related that she did not have enough money, as the journey was long and very expensive. I inquired as to how much she needed, and in British money, it was about fifty pounds. Feeling kind-hearted and generous, I spoke to Shirley, who insisted I give her the finances to meet her needs. We gave her the expenses and a little extra for the journey.

The following morning, I spoke to Madam Zipporah, the matron at the orphanage, expressing my sadness at the situation. "Oh, she said, "Don't let it worry you. That lady's mother dies every week! The same story is told to whoever is here to help us." I had been conned, along with many other visitors to the orphanage before me! I was in great admiration of this quiet, unassuming lady, and her skill to deceive me and so many others!

We went to the local hardware shop with Madam Zipporah, and as I bought plywood to make desks and paint to brighten up the place, I had calculated the price I would have to pay. But upon reaching the desk to pay my bill, I was horrified when he told me that it was almost twice my calculations. Madam Zipporah had bought goods without my knowledge and had asked the man to put them on my bill! Although I was annoyed, African style is African style. As I brought the paint and plywood back to the orphanage, I was excited that the next day, Sandy would make desks and I would begin painting.

The children were wonderful. There were one hundred and twenty, with only one toy between them. They were really happy children, willing to help. I left the paint in a convenient place, and later it was missing. I asked the janitor where he had put my paint, and he pleaded total ignorance as to what I was asking about. He then brought me some white stuff in a bucket, which he said was my paint. It was like milk, and when I showed my annoyance at the situation, this wee man lost his capability to speak English, pleading, "I…no…understand!" That night, with the help of some old technical moves and manoeuvres I had learned as a young man, I picked the lock of his store, and surprise, surprise - there was my paint!

The next day, this man had his English back again! He was very annoyed and angry that I had gone near his store to steal back what he had stolen from me! "I went to the enemy's camp, and I took back what he stole from me" is a wonderful song which would have been very fitting for this occasion!

MINA'S FINAL DAYS

We had to return from Kenya quicker than expected, as Shirley's mother had taken ill with cancer. We were now at Rogart, ministering for the Free Church again. Shirley's mum stayed with us, and they gave her nine months to live if she took treatment. Mina was looking forward to meeting her Saviour, Jesus Christ, rather than delaying the inevitable. Mina was a wonderful woman of faith.

Over that period, we had many visitors as members of the family, and other friends including Jimmy Burney, made the long journey to see Mina. Gilbert and Margaret came up to Rogart on the day they returned from Kenya. The young children from the village who attended a Monday night Christian meeting came to her bedroom window one night and sang to Mina. The whole community supported us at this sad time, but there was much fun and laughter in the midst of it all. Mina had six children, and as Christmas approached, she still had the strength to organise a gift for every member of her family. Everyone was given a Bible; even though some were not Christian believers, there were no exceptions.

Jim especially had a closed heart towards the gospel at that time, and Mina would ask him to read the Bible to her. 1 Corinthians 13 was a favourite. Although he did not verbally object to this request, I am sure there were times he would have chosen a different task. The reading of God's Word was used eventually to bring Jim to Christ. Emotions were different and difficult during this time. Every evening, the family (myself included) would gather around Mina's bed and sing Christmas carols, choruses and hymns. In a quiet and gentle voice, she once told one of her family, "Jesus loves you." The reaction of that person was to cry uncontrollably, and hide themselves in the toilet away from everyone.

You could hear the weeping and sobbing through the door. It is an amazing thing that a woman of God in her final hours of life can carry a sweet and powerful enough anointing that can bring a strong person to a state of brokenness and tears, by gently speaking a revelation of the truth.

On Christmas Day, 2006, we were taking turns to sit with Mina. It was coming late in the evening, and as we reflect on that day, we believe that Mina had run the race and was coming close to finishing the course. From giving out the Bibles in the morning to this time in the evening, she had weakened. Shirley and I were on bedside duty at ten o'clock that night, and we were singing Christian choruses. It had become a normal procedure. Suddenly, Mina sat up in bed and began to sing the chorus, "Because He lives, I can face tomorrow."

I thought that we were witnessing a miracle, and I ran out of the room and along the corridor to the living room to get the rest of the family. Upon returning to the bedroom, Mina was now back in bed and entering a spiritual journey from that bedroom, and this world, into the loving arms of Jesus Christ.

She had arranged her own funeral. Every person taking part was named, and every chorus she wanted sung was sung. She once told me that she had a vision from the Lord that every member of her family would come to know Jesus as their Lord and Saviour, and she died happy, believing this.

HEALED FROM CANCER

After Mina's death, Shirley and I took some time off, although we stayed at Rogart. For about a year, I had tolerated a small abnormal growth on my eyelid. This growth got into my vision, and I needed to cut it several times during that period. I am a DIY enthusiast, and I used a Stanley knife blade to cut it off. Black blood would run out of the wound, and it would settle. I then purchased small wire cutters, which were as good as any surgeon's scalpel. I regularly trimmed this unwelcomed growth. However, with time available, I went to my doctor in Lairg, who made an appointment for me at the Raigmore Hospital in Inverness. A V-shaped cut was made to my eyelid, and I was stitched up and sent home.

A few days later, a phone call came, asking me to go back to the hospital. On meeting the surgeon, he showed concern, feeling my glands and down the side of my face. As I inquired as to the situation, he told me I had a tumour, and it was cancer. Cancer is never a welcome word in a family, and with such a short time since Shirley's mother's death from cancer, I sought a way of telling Shirley the prognosis. The word cancer declares its own prognosis, and arrangements were made for me to go to the Western Infirmary in Glasgow, where my bottom eyelid would be removed entirely and skin brought around to make a false eyelid. I was assured that it could be camouflaged with cosmetics, but it would be very noticeable.

Although I value my good looks, there are some things you have to go through with. Meeting the doctors in the Western Infirmary, they described how they would cut the complete eyelid out and sew skin from the side of my face to make a false eyelid. While accepting my fate, a gentleman in a black suit walked past the doorway, stopped and came back. Asking what was going on, the doctor from Thailand attending to my needs described the situation, and the gentleman in the black suit made a wonderful suggestion. A new drug, in drop form, had just arrived at the hospital. It was like chemotherapy in drop form. If I could administer that (along with two other supporting medications also in drop form), applying this three times a day for nine weeks, they would allow me to leave that day with my eyelid intact. I was to be a guinea pig, but I was happy with whatever. I would get fresh supplies every week, as it had to be refrigerated. I explained that I was a travelling preacher man moving from the Scottish Highlands to the south of Ireland, and they assured me that if I phoned every Friday, advising them of my address, they would have the supplies delivered to me every Monday.

For the next nine weeks, my faithful wife administered the relevant medication, and after this period, with a full-blooded eyeball, I called at the hospital in Glasgow to be told that the medication had worked. I had to have the cancer checked several times, but after some time, I was declared totally healed.

AN ATHEIST IS HEALED

Jim (Mina's son, mentioned earlier) and his wife Ann had lived in Edinburgh for many years, and before Mina's death they had considered moving to the North of Scotland. Jim did not have any time for God in this period of his life. There were reasons for his atheistic beliefs, which are unnecessary to tell at this time.

When he was in Edinburgh, we used to call him "the anti-Christ," as he was strongly opinionated regarding Christian matters. It was easier to take Bibles into China than to bring a Bible into our bedroom when we stayed with him. He had also been poorly at this time, suffering various illnesses. He had stopped working and was physically, emotionally and mentally not well. Some days, he was not able to rise from the settee and had considered suicide but did not have the strength to carry it out. Often, Jim would sit at his mother's bedside, and she would ask him to read a portion of Scripture, which he would do through grated teeth. "Read me that bit in 1 Corinthians 13, Jim. I like that bit. Thank you, Jim." To that request, there was no other solution but to do it.

Jim felt better when he was in the Highlands. It was a quieter and more peaceful life. After Mina passed away, Jim and Ann decided to move north. Shirley and I believed in healing, as well as salvation, and often we would hold meetings in various halls which we rented, and advertised those meetings as Gospel and Healing meetings. On this particular day, we planned a meeting in Lairg, twenty miles from Jim's new home in Golspie.

I received a phone call from Jim asking if he could come to the meeting that evening, and I nearly fell off my seat! I said that would be wonderful, to which he replied that he did not want to go to the meeting but wanted prayer (as he did not believe in that kind of thing, but just in case). The meeting was at 7.30 pm, so I asked him to come at 8.30 pm. The meeting was good, and people were going to be prayed for. Jim came in, physically supported by Ann, his wife. He was shuffling like an old man. He was about fifty-five years of age. He sat at the back, and after we prayed for a few others, we called him forward. I remember Sandy "Lairg" being there, as was George Mackenzie. As we gathered around to pray for Jim, the power of the Lord was present for him to be healed. Although we sensed the power of the Lord, nothing visible happened, and Jim shuffled back to his seat. Shirley's sister, Deirdre, was there that night with Jim and Ann. When they returned to Golspie, Ann had to hold Jim up whilst Deirdre parked the car, and Ann put her house key into the lock. They both helped him upstairs and into bed.

The next morning, as they sat in the living room sharing their disappointment and saying how disappointed Jim must be, there was a sound of someone running down the stairs. And into the living room burst Jim, totally healed. *"But God..."*

It must have been a Sunday morning, as Jim asked who was going to church. At this time, Jim was unsaved. For the next few weeks, he sought the Lord and attended a Tent Meeting in Inverness where I was the speaker for a wonderful ministry called People with a Mission Ministry (PWAMM). They travelled the length and breadth of Scotland with a clear Gospel message that salvation could only be found in the Lord Jesus Christ. At the end of the evening, Jim professed to me that he had asked Jesus for forgiveness of sin and to save him from eternal damnation. A short time later, as Jim pondered over these things, he was unsatisfied with his testimony and wanted to make sure that all things were done decently and in order. He believed that he should openly profess his salvation (Romans 10:10).

One afternoon, in a polytunnel behind his house in Golspie, Sandy Lairg and I were asked to witness the occasion. He knelt on the ground, surrendered his life to Jesus, and wonderfully experienced the evidence of salvation with a peace that passes all understanding. Jim and Ann went on to continue with Jesus, remembering supernatural experiences and close encounters with God.

THE HUNGARIAN EXPERIENCES

We were at a meeting back in Northern Ireland, and a dear friend called Tommy Kennedy asked us if we would like to go on a mission trip to Hungary. I was never one for travelling much: Ireland and Scotland, (along with a few visits to see my daughter in Halesowen, near Birmingham) were sufficient for me. When Tommy asked the question, to my surprise, I answered that I would love to go. We always had an agreement that once you gave your word, you kept it, and I gave my word to Tommy that night that we would go with him on a mission trip to Hungary.

We flew from Dublin and were met in Budapest by a lady called Mella Price. She had a minibus on hire, and on the first night, we were to stay at a cheap hostel in Budapest. The hostel was one big room with men and women sharing the room. Shirley and I grabbed a clean bed, and Tommy and his wife Donna were in a bed next to us, with about a ten-inch gap between the beds.

Sometime through the night, I woke up to find a lovely young lady, standing beside my bed in her underwear! She had descended from a bunk bed next to mine and was preparing to get dressed for an onward journey. This was all a new experience for me. Tommy and Shirley never slept and talked all night; this was our introduction to Hungary.

The following day, we drove to Bag, a village twenty-five miles from Budapest. For the first time in my life, I experienced poverty and the poorest living conditions I had ever encountered. Tommy took out his guitar, and for several hours we sang Christian songs outside their homes. Although they did not speak English, they understood it had Jesus in the middle of the praise and worship. They all professed to be Christians, and even though we did not understand them or their language, Mella could translate a little for us to let them tell us their stories. In such poverty, many children die at birth. Many children also die in their early years, so they have lots of children, as they expect a percentage to die before they grow up. David, a tall, thin man, had eleven children. One lady whom we met was pregnant, and the next time we called, they told us she had died in childbirth. This was something that was a common occurrence, and finding out you were pregnant could be a death sentence.

Later that day, we drove to Debrecen. Debrecen is the second largest city in Hungary. We came to a tall building which had been built in the communist era. It was a block of flats with two to three thousand people living there. We were going to meet some Christians Mella had known, and she wanted to introduce them to us. We went up several flights of stairs until we came to an apartment. Entering it, we found that the kitchen was very small, and the largest room in the flat was the bedroom. The place was packed out.

There was a large bed in the room, and people were sitting in the middle and on the sides of the bed. This large number of people were waiting for us and expecting us to bring blessings of worship and teaching from God's Word. I was primed to share something, but with no capable translator, how could we move on? All of a sudden, a young man appeared at the door. No one knew him, and he knew no one there. "I don't know what I am doing here," he said in perfect English.

We began to speak to him and found out that he was a translator, able and capable of translating from English into Hungarian and vice-versa. We were all so excited, believing that God had sent this young man. We spent the next few hours praising and worshipping God, and the people received the Word of the Lord with gladness. Later, we considered if this young man was an angel in disguise. By the time we left, there was no sign of him anywhere.

Our next stop was Nyirbeltek, to meet with Kati and Danny. Kati was a character, a strong woman whom you would not dare to mess with. Although they were both considered to be pastors, Kati was the person in charge. Danny played the accordion and never preached or spoke very much. They both had a good grasp of the English language, which made life easier for us. We stayed in a building near them which they had bought for a church some years earlier. Danny was very practical and had fixed up the building to a good standard. We held several meetings there, and God moved in mighty ways with salvation, healings, and deliverance at almost every meeting. Some people were hearing the Scriptures for the first time and were renouncing their involvement in witchcraft and other occultic practices, accepting Christ as Saviour and Lord.

TAKING AID TO HUNGARY

Coming back from our first trip to Hungary, we were saddened at the poverty and deprivation in so many of the smaller villages. People there say that many come as "poor's tourists." They go to see the poverty, take pictures, show them in their churches upon their return, and never go back or make any effort to help. We did not want to be "poor's tourists" and began to organise the collection of goods and transportation to take goods to the poor in Hungary. We organised a lorry load from Northern Ireland. Jim, Shirley's brother, organised one from Scotland.

The two lorries arrived at the same time, and Danny and Kati had a big garden surrounded by a high-security fence. They also had a guard dog, as break-ins and theft are a serious problem in certain villages. We were therefore able to unload the lorries and leave the goods in the garden until we sorted it out the following day. There was furniture, medical goods, clothes, blankets, food, sweets, beds and mattresses. It was simply amazing.

The weather was about thirty degrees centigrade, and the next day, all these people came from local villages. They had wheelbarrows and carts, and goods of every description were being carried away to their homes. I remember one time visiting a house where there was an old man, and the only furniture in the house consisted of a hard dining room chair, where he sat all day. I prayed that he had received a comfortable, soft chair where he could sit for the rest of his life.

We were to visit Danny and Kati many times during the twelve years we did mission trips to Hungary and Romania. Later on, we brought many lorry loads of goods to various other churches and places in Hungary, Romania, and Ukraine. In those small villages, witchcraft was a very prominent religion. We would often have experiences of resistance to the Gospel being preached and resistance to our programmes and plans, but we continued unabated.

Occasionally, we would be woken up in the middle of the night by a drum beating. We were told this was to call upon their ancestral spirits to come and visit the area. We would simply pray. Kati had a strong ministry in deliverance, and you could find some demon-possessed people being set free in many of our meetings and accepting the salvation of the Lord. Many of the meetings we held were outside.

At one of those meetings in Hajduhadhaz, we were crammed into an old, corrugated iron shed. I was the preacher, and near the end of the message I saw a woman coming towards me through the crowd. She was obviously demonised, and her intentions were to harm me. She was crawling like a snake on the earthen floor. She was snarling and foaming at the mouth, and although we had experienced demonic possession many times, this was at a level we had not previously encountered. This woman meant business. With authority, I spoke in English, a language she would not understand, and simply said, "Jesus," in a firm, commanding voice. She backed off as if she had met a lion and collapsed on the ground. Later on that evening, Christian leaders brought her to renounce her Satanic worship and to find salvation in Jesus. She was completely set free.

Another night in Hajduhadhaz, we went with the lovely Christmas boxes that many make up, filled with all manner of goodies. We had been told the number of children in the village, and we filled the car with Christmas boxes, bringing a few extra just in case. The pastor there was Miklos, and he was co-ordinating things. We went into the backyard of a house, and big gates were closed behind us. We had Danny with us. He was the only one who could translate for us. The crowd gathered around, pushing and shoving. There was a bad atmosphere in the place, and we were a little concerned for our safety.

It was extremely unsettling. Here we were with hundreds of poor gypsies, and no one in the world knew where we were. We had been attacked before and had to abandon the trailer we had in another village, which had several hundred Christmas boxes in it. Eventually, there was a settling, and we came out of the car to distribute the boxes. A woman came in behind us and stole a box, and I went after her, grabbing back our box and shouting at her. The atmosphere changed again, and we felt in danger. Danny pleaded for the gates to be opened, and outside was another crowd, who had been made aware of what was happening and did not want to miss their opportunity to receive a gift. In the end, we sat in the car, and the gates were eventually opened. With a foot on the accelerator, we made a bid to escape. We made it out without being killed or killing anyone.

Some children had never received a present in their lives.

Distributing Christmas boxes was an amazing experience. If we saw people beside the road, we would stop, give them a box, and take off, looking in the mirror to see their surprised faces. One time, we stopped at a bus stop and gave everyone standing there a Christmas box. There was no communication between us, but we loved the surprise element.

A BROKEN CURSE AND THE BLIND SEE

We brought several lorries loaded with goods to Nyirbeltek, and met various and different people every time we went. One time there, we again stayed at the church building, where a team from Budapest was evangelising. They called themselves Adullam Ministries. When you went to the villages, you always found someone who wanted to trust the Lord as their Saviour. You saw people being healed, and you saw people delivered from evil spirits.

This particular evening, the gentlemen from Adullam Ministries, along with Shirley and I, decided to go to different villages. We had an exciting time and saw some wonderful things that God had done. On our return, the Adullam Ministries men were rejoicing and shouting and praising God. In the village they went to, there were two children who were blind from birth. A certain witch had cursed the family, and upon hearing this, the leader of Adullam Ministries, a man called Chubba, cried to the Lord in prayer, breaking the curse of witchcraft in Jesus' name. Instantly, the two children received their sight back to twenty-twenty vision. We rejoiced with them and have many stories of God moving in great power amongst the poor in Eastern Europe.

A GYPSY WEDDING

Danny and Kati, pastors of the church at Nyirbeltek, were sent a tent from Northern Ireland. It was as new, and it was decided to have a tent mission. I was to be the speaker, and after preaching, as you do in those villages, you ask if anyone wants to be saved, Baptised in the Holy Spirit, healed, or delivered. You address the people through the help of a translator.

A young lady called Christina came forward and told us of the continuous pain in her stomach area. After we prayed for healing, we began to pray for deliverance, whereby Christina was set free from something demonic and was marvellously healed. There was no problem in leading this young lady to Jesus for salvation. Christina lived with her boyfriend Laszlo, but as we say, he was a common-law husband. As she would have no other place to stay, we did not speak about the situation, but on another night of the mission, her man came with her. They sat beside each other. Christina seldom smiled, as her two front teeth were missing, but you could tell she was happy that he had come with her. At the end, the usual call went out for souls wanting to be saved, people to receive healing and others to receive deliverance. Who stepped out of the seat? Laszlo, Christina's man! Accepting Jesus through a sinner's prayer, he went back to his seat.

Christina was so pleased for him, and I guess also for herself. I then approached the subject of them living together, which is a common situation. I told them that they were both saved, and they should be married, and almost immediately Laszlo and Christina were standing in front of me. When I asked the translator what they wanted, she told me that they wanted me to marry them. I tried to explain about paperwork, and that we needed it to make things official. We agreed that the next time we came, we would bring a bridal dress and a suit for Laszlo.

The next time we went, bringing another lorry load of aid, we had the wedding dress donated to us by Ruth MacAskill from Glenelg in Scotland. It was beautiful and sequenced. And when Shirley brought it to Christina, it fitted like a glove.

Laszlo and Christina on their wedding day.

The big day came. Shirley was bridesmaid and I was the best man. Kati officiated. Our car was the wedding car, as there was only one other car in that village, and it was a right old banger. We made tables from rotten floorboards and put them inside the tent. A huge pot of Hungarian Goulash was cooked over an outside fire, and the wedding ceremony went ahead without a hitch. Although I did not see any paperwork, it was the first "official" wedding in that village, or the surrounding villages, in living memory. No one had ever been to a wedding, and the excitement went on for days.

LIFE-CHANGING SITUATION

Another time we brought a load of aid and goods. This consignment contained some televisions, and Danny took control of the distribution of these precious items. Analogue terrestrial television reception was changing in the UK to Digital, around 2012, and many were buying new televisions. The old transmission was on UHF 625 lines, and many television sets were defunct in the UK but would work in Hungary and Romania. We visited a home in Csenger on the border between Hungary and Romania. This couple were Christians, but full of religious nonsense.

They had a beautiful daughter around eighteen years old, and a son who was a little younger. The daughter looked depressed, even suicidal, with her hope almost gone. Her mother was overbearing. They had no television, radio, or any other item to pass away the times. Knowing that Danny had taken receipt of those televisions, we went back to get one. To our surprise, Danny was reluctant to give us one. Eventually, he relented, and we headed back to Csenger to bring a television to this family. We stopped at a Tesco shop on the journey and bought an aerial. We also bought a radio and CD player for the boy. When we arrived, we were welcomed, but it was nothing compared to the joy the children showed when we brought in the television and the radio/CD player. After setting up the television, we went to fix the radio/CD player and realised we had no CDs. Searching the car, we found a CD of Susan Boyle, who had been on the TV show, "Britain's Got Talent."

When I returned to the house, the young girl was shouting, "Susan Boyle! Susan Boyle! Susan Boyle!" To this day, we cannot understand how she knew of Susan Boyle, but we believe that we changed the lives of those two young people. We were blessed to have helped change the lives of many individuals and families, orphanages, and schools over the years as we brought aid to Eastern Europe.

THE POWER OF THE SPIRIT

Danny was a quiet man, but Kati on the other hand was a real powerful woman of God. She had a tremendous anointing for deliverance, and needed to have, as she often worked in villages where demonic forces were a reality. One of the most amazing meetings I have ever had the privilege to attend was organised by Danny and Kati. I do not know the name of the village we were at; all I know is that the hall where they met had been an old communist gymnasium at one time.

The seats were the old benches you used for step-ups. Everything surrounding us was concrete and a concrete grey colour, with climbing frames on the walls. The meeting began, and I was the preacher. They are always delighted to have someone from the West coming to one of their meetings. They have some false idea that we are Godlier than they are, and at times you would need to be careful that you did not become an idol to worship.

The meeting went on, and I was up at the front to preach. I remember being very far away from the people gathered that evening. Kati was the translator. It was going as well as I expected, when all of a sudden, a person walked into this big grey room and the atmosphere changed. I believe that it was the person of the Holy Spirit of God. I looked around and saw that something was happening, and whatever the situation, I was no longer the person in charge. People began to weep, some falling to their knees. Others fell off the seat, falling backwards. I stood and watched in total amazement, at what I now know was the Holy Spirit working in the hearts of men and women, and these were the effects of His power and amazing presence. It was very powerful, yet very gentle, and very effective.

A lady stepped forward for prayer. Kati explained to me she had suffered migraine headaches all her life, and asked if could I pray for her. She was some yards away from me, and as I began to walk over to her, this supernatural power knocked her to the floor. Her head bounced on the hard concrete floor, and I can still see it in my mind's eye. I remember saying to the Lord, that she wanted healed Lord, not killed. Later, she came out of her trance and staggered like a drunk person, testifying that all the pain was gone. She was freed from the migraine headaches, we believe, forever.

TELEVISIONS FOR THE PRISONERS

We often headed for Oradea in Romania after being at Danny and Kati's, where we had made friends with Bob and Caroline Schmitz, who were the pastors at the Church of God in Oradea. Bob was an American gentleman, and Caroline was from Paisley, Scotland. We became friends and we took several loads of aid to them there, where they were distributed to the poor. The televisions I wrote about in an earlier chapter were very plentiful in Scotland and Northern Ireland, but were now useless there, as they were out of date.

One day, as we visited a prison in Oradea, we were asked if we could get some televisions for the prisoners. They would not let them watch any programme they wanted, as it was censored by the prison office, and certain harmless programmes were made available to watch every day. Knowing the situation of so many television sets being useless in the UK and being scrapped, we made an agreement with the prison Governor that if the prisoners were allowed to watch an hour of Christian programmes several times a week, we would get them televisions. The request was granted, and on our next visit, we brought a whole lot of television sets to the prison, and we pray that the prison Governor kept his promise. When you consider the timing and the whole situation, you have to say: *"But God..."*

GOD'S SMUGGLERS

There was a time when we wanted to take Christmas boxes to Kati and Danny to be distributed to the children in various villages. We arranged to hire a big van and went to Arad in Romania to collect the boxes, as that was the distribution point. The journey would take us over four hours from Arad to Nyirbeltek. We filled the lorry and headed north to Nyirbeltek, past Oradea, and headed for the Hungarian border. There are many checkpoints at the Romanian/Hungarian border, which we were aware of, but for some reason (possibly the excitement) we headed for Hungary without having the necessary documentation. We also got lost trying to get to the border in an area we were unsure of. Finally, we came to the border at Létavértes.

At the border, the guard stopped us, as per usual. "Papers please," one asked. I gave him the papers for the vehicle, but it was papers for the consignment he was looking for. He was looking for the manifest of the goods we were carrying. "Open please," was his next request, and here was a lorry load of Christmas boxes without any official papers, to enter Hungary. The atmosphere was not pleasant as they thought we were smugglers, and that we were doing drugs or alcohol behind those boxes. They spoke very little English, and we knew even less Hungarian.

At the point of our arrest, a tall man wearing a Russian Cossack hat came on the scene. He spoke perfect English. He inquired of the situation, and the border guards wanted an arrest to be made immediately. However, he was calm and took out a couple of big boxes which contained the smaller Christmas boxes. Upon examination, he asked if we had any other goods, to which we replied that this was it. It was now coming up to ten o'clock at night, it was dark, and we were getting very tired. This dear man with the Russian Cossack hat gave us clearance and released us to continue our journey. We arrived with Danny and Kati, and after emptying the lorry we enjoyed the comforts of a bedroom that night and not a prison cell.

IMRE KOSZTA

One day we got a phone call from a man called Imre Koszta. Imre asked for our help. He helped many villages inside Romania near the Hungarian border. The people identified as Hungarian and spoke Hungarian because after the First World War, when borders were realigned, those people had been displaced and lived in poverty, with neither the Romanian government willing to help, or the Hungarian government allowed to help. Although we had met Imre at Danny and Kati's house and other meetings, we really did not know him.

He had been an ordained Hungarian Reformed minister, but the church was not meeting the needs of the poor. He and his wife Maria would make sandwiches with bread, margarine and salami and go to the villages to feed the poor. Eventually, he packed in the ministry of a normal minister, as it was too sanitized for Imre, and did not serve the needs of the poor. He was supported by a charity from the Netherlands. He worked with the poor in many villages along the border between Hungary and Romania. Imre was a flamboyant man, with a lot of charisma, and was loved by the poor in the villages. He was their source of life on many occasions and in many circumstances.

He had a motto which allowed him to sail very close to the wind, in relation to the Romanian laws, which at times was necessary. That motto was "Doing things for the greater good of humanity." We could not object to that, as the paperwork we used for twelve years to cross the border into Romania was not as official as it should have been, or as official as they thought it was. We were told that the communist mindset is, that if there are sufficient red ink stamps on the paperwork, then it had to be official.

Officially, we would have been required to take our goods to a registered charity in Romania that had previously sent us a letter and requested the consignment. If you did that, half the goods needed for the poor would simply go missing. Such rubbish as officialdom was not really necessary and was ignored for the greater good of humanity. At times, a man at the border who was short in stature, would become very officious, going through our shipment and say to me, 'I am very suspicious of you." I would smile and think to myself that he had every reason to be suspicious of us! If only he knew!

THE POOR VILLAGES

The villages we helped were poor. It is beyond my ability to describe how poor they really were. The average mortality age was less than forty years of age. It was not through illness, but through lack of good food, vitamins, minerals, and nutrition when they were children. The lack of vitamins and minerals in their diet was evident in the colours in their hair (some being bronze when the colour should have been jet black). The children were dirty and many were naked in the summer months. Many were hungry on a daily basis.

Now and again, we would see a young child who was blonde, and we were told that a mother would sell herself to a passing lorry driver for five euros, to enable her to feed the children. The houses were in a terrible condition. Hygiene was non-existent. Most houses were built of clay and straw and the walls became a haven for rats to nest in and reproduce. The rats would bite the children in the night hours. The rats drank from the same dirty well as the villagers, and often there were illnesses and deaths that were directly attributed to these rodents.

We were able to pay for boring wells in some villages. Now they have clean water to drink from a hand-operated pump. Washing themselves is not a big priority. The village of Silindru was the worst we had seen. The lack of our ability to alleviate their poverty to a sufficient level left us standing, weeping and crying, frustrated and at times angry with ourselves. Angry at the injustice of it all, I would stand in the middle of the village looking to Heaven for guidance. Silindru was the place we called the village at the end of the world.

In Silindru and other villages, we built houses for the really poor. They were eight metres long by four metres wide by two point four metres to the ceiling. They initially cost three thousand pounds and with our wonderful supporters we built many houses, two churches and a few boreholes for water during the twelve years we were privileged to help there, as well as bringing all manner of goods and clothing. The decision as to who got a house was made on the basis of whether their children were taken from them and into an orphanage as a result of the bad living conditions. When the house was built, they would get their children back, so our decision was never too hard to make. At times, the house we built for a family would have been sold to another family for a very small sum of money or exchanged for a horse and cart the next time we would visit. At times this was heart-breaking, but it was part of their culture and you had to accept some of these traits which were part of their lives. They simply thought differently from us.

This is a picture of a girl we called Lotzie, one of our favourite children. Her real name was Melinda, and we watched her grow year by year.

This is an extremely poor house where several children lived.

This is the inside of an average poor home

This would be an average poor village. The house on the right-hand side
with a red roof is one we built.

This is an example of the houses we built.

DYING LIKE AN ANIMAL

A man in one of the villages died when we were there. He was about forty years old, and upon asking if there would be a funeral service, Imrie told us that it was not the way they did things in the poor villages. "You see," he said "This man was never registered as born. He had no identity as a human being, no birth certificate no rights to education, no rights to the health service, no identification card, nothing. In a world of officialdom, he did not exist. A hole will be dug for him to be buried in, because he never *was*, as far as the authorities know." If a child is born into a poor family, they do not register that child and if they do, the social services will come and see that the poverty is too great for them to leave the child in such impoverished conditions. The child will be taken to an orphanage, where later on, he or she could be abused or ill-treated.

Not registering a child does not allow the child to have rights to education, or access to health services, although we would see this changing as the years went on. It was generally young boys we would see coming back from having attended school in the villages. The gypsy encampments were generally just outside a Romanian village, allowing them to have access to the shops and other amenities, and the men would sometimes get some work.

This is a perfect example of the new house that replaced the house on the right.

THE POWER OF PRAYER

On the gospel front, we went to many villages to share the Good News. It was interesting to have a revelation of the power of prayer. One morning, we went to a certain village. The people were wild, with the women doing that shrilling noise you would hear Indians (First Nations) make in the cowboy films. That year, we had filled black bags with a mixture of clothes and blankets, as well as some food. As we distributed these goods, the women (more so than the men) began to fight and pull the bags from one another, and the contents of the bags were strewn all over the ground. We were grateful that Imre was with us, as he carried some authority with those wild people.

The next village we visited was so different. They accepted their bags of clothes peacefully and quietly with gratitude, yet the two villages were only a matter of a few miles apart. We asked Imre why the people were so different, to which he replied: "We have a few Christian praying women in this village, and we are making inroads with the Gospel. The first village has not received the Gospel as yet, but soon we will begin a work there also." It was an amazing insight into the power of prayer. We saw that the very atmosphere in a village was different through the power of prayer. Imre told us that the two villages were very similar when he first began to visit them.

A CHRISTMAS MIRACLE

Sometimes, when on mission, people see miracles, and no matter how you try to explain it, it is clearly the hand of God. One Christmas time we were in Hungary and Romania with a lorry load of aid and many thousands of Christmas boxes. There was snow on the ground and a heavy frost that year, making the roads treacherous. Although we had received some of our consignment, more shoeboxes were coming on another lorry. As a result of the road conditions, that particular lorry took a detour, and our Christmas boxes ended up in Arad, around a three-hour journey away (and that would be in good weather).

We had an ex-military man with us that year, and after he made a risk assessment, he declared it too dangerous and unwise to travel. Shirley and Deirdre refused to accept his assessment, as they saw this as a bit of excitement and a challenge rather than a danger. So, off we went and found the lorry carrying our boxes in Arad. Packing our car and hired minibus, we made the journey on ice-covered roads. On collection of our second load that day, we told the lorry driver that we would not be back until the next morning. He told us he was very sorry but he needed the lorry emptied before night-time came. The lorry was a curtain-sider, and thieves would cut the sides if goods were left in it. He phoned someone who was only too willing to benefit from our situation, but we were four hundred and fifty boxes short. All the boxes were assigned to various pastors, orphanages and children's homes, and we were short.

It was coming near Christmas day. Shirley and I were the only ones left on the mission field, but hoped to be back in the UK by Christmas Day. Imre was not pleased that we had promised what we could not fulfil. It is an Eastern European attitude that you are to blame whatever the situation. We could tell he had made promises, and on the strength of our promise, he too, would look bad for failing to keep his word.

It was the twenty-first of December, and hopes of helping the situation were impossible. We did not even pray about the situation, as it was so impossible to get or even buy four hundred and fifty Christmas boxes. On a previous occasion, we had bought one thousand boxes from a Baptist Church in Oradea for two hundred pounds, but even that was not possible at this late stage,

It was the afternoon when a friend (a lady called Fiona Kelly from Rasharkin, Northern Ireland) phoned. Fiona is also involved in charity work and sends many thousands of Christmas boxes to the poor every year. "Donald,' she said. 'I have four hundred and fifty shoeboxes left over from our load. Could you use them?" "Use them?" I said, "They will stop World War Three from beginning!" "Are you sure it's four hundred and fifty boxes?" I asked in disbelief. "Yes," said Fiona, not knowing our predicament. "Exactly four hundred and fifty." Fiona arranged an overnight delivery service, and two pallets were delivered on the twenty-third of December, with four hundred and fifty shoeboxes and other boxes of good, warm clothing. Thank you, Jesus. We were back in the UK for Christmas. Mission accomplished. What can you say? *"BUT GOD..."*

FUNDATIA VIS DE COPIL

On another occasion, we left Berettyoujfalu in Hungary, where our store was, and headed to Oradea, then onwards to Timisoara, passing Arad. Timisoara was a four-hour journey away. We planned to stay in a hotel that night in Timisoara. There were times you needed to stay in a hotel so you could have a shower or bath, a good clean up and a day away from it all. Hotels in Romania were cheap at that time, and you could get a double room for thirty euros, including a good breakfast.

Before we left, we filled the car with various items we had left in the store with the intention of giving them to someone we may meet. There was a pushchair for a child, warm clothes for children, health drinks and other odd things with which we filled the car. Little did we know that the following day we would call in a café in Arad for a cup of coffee and a cake, and meet a lovely lady from Glasgow. Her name was Kathryn, and along with her family, they ran Fundatia Vis de Copil ("A Child's Dream") and their desire was to simply help the poor. Their property was used by homeless people and ladies of the night to wash themselves, as well as other people going through hard times.

When people called, they would always show them hospitality and kindness, no matter what their occupation or situation. Kathryn had heard us speaking in English, and she sent the waiter to inquire as to where we were from. We were introduced to one another. She told us a little of her work, and we told her our reason for being there. We asked her if she had any needs, and she began to make a list. Every item she listed we had in our car (even the health drinks she needed for a very sick man she knew, and apparently, such health drinks were not to be found in Romania at the time). Surely the hand of God was upon the work. I can honestly say that the list was exactly what we had in the car. *But God..."*

SLOVAKIA AND UKRAINE

Although we enjoyed being in Hungary and Romania, we also enjoyed exploits into Slovakia and Ukraine. Whilst in Killarney in the South of Ireland, we had met this lovely family called Rutka (Ruth), her sister Noemi, Noemi's husband Peter and their son Brian. They were from Slovakia and were making and saving money whilst working in Ireland to improve their lives back home.

We had been asked to run the Living Rock Church at Killarney as Pastor Michael and his family visited his wife Nympha's family (she was also known as Indai) in the Philippines. The Living Rock Church had seventeen different nationalities at the time, and this Slovakian family were professing Christians who attended that church. Getting to know them was a privilege, and they said, "If you are ever in Slovakia, call in and see us; we live in a small village called Medzianky." You know how people always say that if you are ever in their country to come and see them! One day, we were in Hungary. We didn't have Google Maps or sat-nav help available to us, so we looked up the map and found this little town on a Slovakian map.

We were a three-hour drive from the village of Medziank, so off we went to find Rutka and Noemi. Three hours later, we were coming down the wee road leading to the house we were looking for. Oh, the excitement was tremendous. This family had a lovely house. Vera, their mother, had spent a year in the USA sewing American flags from morning to bedtime, to save enough money to repair the house. Pavel the father, went to Italy and picked apples to earn wages, as work in that area of Slovakia is hard to find. Within a few minutes, we were sitting at a table, with Rutka translating for us, and living in that house were four generations of the one family. They had no riches, but what they had they shared generously. They were not poor in provisions, as they had a garden with choice vegetables and fruit, and they also kept goats for meat for special occasions. We visited Pavel, Viera and the family on several occasions. There we would preach in their church, the pastor giving you a chapter to read and his sermon to preach. Although we were "loosed" on many occasions, the church was run very strictly, and trusting a Pentecostal in the pulpit was just too much for this pastor! That was until one evening, the pastor's daughter got Baptised in the Holy Spirit, and life for the pastor changed, having seen the amazing transformation that took place in her life.

On one occasion, during a visit to Pavel and Vera's home, I was walking past the pens where the goats were kept. There was a baby goat, a kid goat, not that old. As I watched them in the pen, I said to Pavel that the kid goat was very nice. Pavel replied, "You like Donald - you like?" "Yes, Pavel, very nice," I said. Pavel got the idea that I liked the kid goat to eat, and a few days later, that poor goat was on my plate for dinner, sliced and cut up with vegetables and potatoes!

HUNGARIAN FISH AND CHIPS

One of the loads of aid we brought to Hungary was to a village near Tiszafüred on the Tisza River. The river had flooded its banks and people were in great need, especially of household furniture. The minister of the Hungarian Reformed Church was a lovely man, and the people in the village were so blessed and grateful for our help. The pastor was Rev. Fazekas, and his brother is a minister in the Isle of Skye. He and his wife were lovely people who really cared for their congregation and for others in the village. He was also a national poet and a very intelligent man.

To show their appreciation for the help that Highways Byways Mission had been to them, they asked Shirley what my favourite food was, as they wanted to cook a meal for us. Shirley told them that I was partial to fish and chips, and one evening we were invited to their home for a "fish supper." Excitement and anticipation filled the air, and soon, sitting in front of me was this fish. It still had the head and the tail on, and this eye was watching me! I took its head off to make sure it was dead, and after removing some of the scales, I found that the inside was black. He insisted Shirley and I eat up, and Shirley, being more adventurous than I am with such things as food, was soon eating little bits. I was attacking the chips, and this eye, now sitting at the side of the plate, was still watching me. As I looked at the minister's plate, he had eaten it all, including the head and tail, making swallowing sounds as he sucked at the eyes. I eventually had to make some excuse to pardon myself, and I persuaded the dear minister to eat mine as well as his own!

Food was always a trial for me when travelling, and I often took a big bottle of HP sauce to kill the taste of some of the dishes set before us! Another time, I was eating what I thought were mushrooms, only to find out they were chicken hearts. Even in that situation, the HP sauce had no effect!

HLINNE, SLOVAKIA

During our visit to this area, we met up with Pierre and Lisa. They were missionaries to the gypsies, and their main church was at Hlinne. Their mission is the Word for the World, and they are involved in Bible translation into gypsy languages, as well as other projects.

The first night I preached with Pierre translating was at Hlinne. Hlinne was a gypsy village, and the local church had been built there. The church was packed out. Expectations were high, and there was great excitement. As I came to the end of my message, I asked for a response to the Gospel. Almost everyone in the house came running forward, weeping and crying in repentance and joy. As they knelt on their hands and knees, small pools of tears were visible on the tiled floor.

We prayed with many for salvation, healing and deliverance. We asked Pierre and Lisa as to the reality of the decisions made, to be told that the following morning, Pierre would drive around the village. If there was washing on the fence, or a door or gate was newly painted, and the place had been tidied up, then salvation had come to that home. They did not know why this happened, but Pierre believed that being cleansed by the precious Blood of the Lamb of God, everything felt dirty around them, and needed to be washed or painted.

We had many wonderful nights in Slovakia, sometimes just gathered around the big family table at Pavel and Vera's house or in a gypsy village up on the top of mountains.

One night, we crammed into a building. I was preaching, with Pierre translating. We were in full flow when a baby was lifted over the seats and handed to this big lady in the front row (if there was a front row). I continued to preach. I was focused on my message when, all of a sudden, the top of this lady's shirt was opened, and she began to breastfeed the child. There are times on mission when you need to try to understand culture, but my shocked face seemed to make many laugh, and it was difficult to concentrate and keep focused on preaching in such a situation. I decided to cut my sermon short and give the meeting back to Pierre, who suggested we should sing a few more songs and then close the meeting.

VISITING UKRAINE

On one occasion, we travelled from Pavel and Vera's house to meet up with a pastor in Ukraine. We were warned that the area we were to visit was very poor, and should we be kidnapped or robbed or our car was taken from us, we would have no come-back, as the criminals were mafia, the police were mafia, and the judges were mafia. So, our chances of being seen again were very limited. We were often asked if we were wise, and at times, being wise is not what is required to get the work done!

We were passing time as we were waiting for a delivery of a lorry load of aid. We got Gordon Black from Cookstown to bring the goods to Nyirbeltek in Hungary. From Slovakia, we could cross into Ukraine and back into Hungary, so it all seemed to be a sensible plan. Gordon had asked us to take the payment for the transportation with us in cash and pay him in Hungary, as he would have concerns about being robbed en route. The cost was three thousand pounds, and we had this in our car. As we approached the Ukrainian border, I decided to hide a few of our private possessions in a place under the gear lever which looked safe, and I forgot about the money. We were made to wait for well over an hour, although the place was not busy.

Guards with big dogs marched from one building to another, and we were made to feel very vulnerable, especially in a car from the United Kingdom, Also, being a right-hand drive, great interest was being shown in the car. Eventually, we were called forward. Sniffer dogs smelled the door panels, and the guards looked through our luggage. "Any whiskey?" one asked. "Any cigarettes?" We were advised to place a twenty-euro bill on the dashboard. If they asked for it, you gave it; if they did not ask, you did not offer it. After a period of time, we were cleared to continue our journey, only to find every traffic sign was in Ukrainian and our map was in English.

We decided that we could never find the pastor we wanted to meet, so we cancelled that idea. Driving into the unknown, we found ourselves coming to another border, but this one was taking us back into Slovakia (but we had planned to be at the Hungarian border). I was the driver, and on seeing the border guards with guns, we made a handbrake turn on the road, expecting to hear shots from a rifle, but we got away and eventually made it back into Hungary. Remembering the money, I panicked and asked Shirley where the money was. Shirley patted her chest and assured me that the money was safely stuffed into her bra!

I think there could have been work available for her as a smuggler or some kind of secret agent with MI5. It must have been tips she picked up watching James Bond!

ROMANIAN GYPSY CHURCH

In Hungary and Romania, our mission was more in line with helping the poor rather than on a spiritual level, although we did have some amazing moments, like some we have already recorded. In a gypsy village in Romania, I was speaking in a church that was full of hungry souls. There were, at that time, some moves of God amongst the gypsies. You were never short of translators in Romania, as they wanted to improve their English and used every opportunity to do so.

This certain church was waiting with bated breath for the preacher to begin, and after preaching for a certain amount of time, I made the usual request for those whom the Gospel message affected and wished to give their hearts to Jesus. As I did this, a man at the back started shouting at people and pointing at them. Those he pointed to came forward for prayer. I inquired of my translator about the meaning of this, and he told me that the man shouting and pointing was a prophet, and he was directing who could and could not come forward, believing that he was getting direct revelation from Heaven.

As this situation was happening, I was led to call young people and children to surrender their hearts to Christ. There was a sudden commotion as young people, and parents with young children, and mothers carrying their babies, came forward to respond to the invitation to come to Christ. As we prayed a sinner's prayer together, many wept openly, and young children, with their heads bowed in sincerity, sobbed quietly at the front of the building as I looked over them from a raised pulpit. It was a moment with God. This church was under the authority of the Romanian Pentecostal Church, which, to me, is a bit controlling.

After the meeting, I was reprimanded for calling children and young people to respond, as they believe they cannot get saved until they are fifteen years of age. They believe that to be truly saved, you need to be baptised, and you cannot be baptised until you are fifteen. Personally speaking, I believe that many of the children and young people were gloriously saved that morning, despite the teaching of the church.

ANOTHER JEHOVAH JIREH

The provision of finances to carry out the work we were doing was miraculous, to say the least. One couple generously supported us on a monthly basis for many years, and for a short period of time a church gave a monthly donation. But the miracle of provision was given from the hand of God through whoever he prompted to support us.

Looking back on the financial side of our work in Eastern Europe, we cannot but feel blessed to remember God's providential care and provision. Without a doubt, His hand was on the work and on our lives. We had been able to build homes for the poor. We helped build two churches, and at the time of writing, we are supporting the building of another new church in Romania. We had sunk boreholes for water. We had paid for the transportation of lorry loads of aid to Hungary and Romania and supported pastors and church leaders to improve their facilities and their own lives and living conditions.

One night in Frankfurt, Germany, coming back to the UK from Slovakia, we stopped at a motorway service station for a bed for the night as the heavens had opened, and the rain came down in torrents. It was hard to see, as the window wipers were not keeping up with the lashing rain. A lovely, well-spoken Englishman came over to us and asked if he could buy a meal for us. Explaining that our need was more a bed than food, we politely declined. Inquiring about our reasons for being in Frankfurt, we explained what we did in helping the poor and above all, we were Christian evangelists of sorts. He was a lovely gentleman and seemed genuinely interested. He asked if we had a business card which at that time we did, and after what was a maximum of five minutes, we parted company.

Sometime later, I got an email from this man whose name was David. He wanted to donate to the work and asked if we wanted a cheque or bank transfer. We had made inquiries about this man on the internet, and it all seemed above board. We sent him our bank details, expecting a maximum donation of about fifty pounds, when we learned that he had donated one thousand pounds into our account. Encounters like this were common. On another occasion, we wanted to buy a shipping container to store the goods we collected for the poor. A container at that time would cost three thousand pounds. We were praying about the situation when a man walked in and said he and his wife had heard we wanted to buy a container, and they wanted to pay for it.

In all honesty, we do not know who told them, as the only people who knew our plans were Shirley and I, and one other. I guess that God knew, and here was another situation where we say, *"But God..."* These are just two of the amazing stories of God's provision, and we are humbled to say that never in all the years we have been in ministry or on the mission field have we asked for money, or organised anything to raise funds.

God has provided for us every step of the way. When we bought the container, we needed to put the electricity cable underground, as it would be too near the container when overhead. We needed to hire a crane to have the container lifted over a wall to get it in the proper position on our ground, and there were many other expenses which we calculated would be in the region of six thousand pounds at the time. But every need that we had was fully met by God's provision. You can understand why we say, *"But God..."*

BACK IN NORTHERN IRELAND

As the years rolled on, we found ourselves back in Northern Ireland in March 2012 after Shirley's uncle died, leaving a widow and no children. Jim and Esther had been robbed at gunpoint some years earlier, and living out in the country brought concern about her safety and well-being, which was being expressed by Shirley's brothers and sisters. Shirley and I decided that we would spend the rest of that year with Esther, and provide a bit of security and company for her in the winter months.

Our base was now in Northern Ireland, and we continued to collect goods for Eastern Europe with the help of John and Doreen Greenaway, who graciously gave us an insulated polytunnel to gather, sort and send the goods to their destination. It involved hard work and long hours collecting goods from throughout the country, but during this time, we were also out preaching and teaching at house meetings and local churches. We also took the odd run over to our friends Louise and Rosemary, who live in Donegal. They organised meetings in their home, where we would preach and pray with people. We also took a few runs down to Killarney, staying with Theresa Loughlin, who showed us great kindness.

Another family who were exceptionally kind to us, were the Burney family in Armagh. Jimmy and Nora had a couple of meetings in their home every month, and John Purcell and I shared the preaching. At many of those meetings we met many interesting characters, some with a chequered history, but now professing salvation. Jimmy and Nora became close friends, as did John and Patricia Purcell. John and I did a mission at the Mourne Country Hotel in Newry over a two-night period. Posters approximately three feet by two feet were placed around the town and at roundabouts in the area.

People came from all over, and a large crowd gathered. We sang some favourite choruses, and then preached a straight-talking Gospel message. Hell was mentioned many times as something to be fearful of, and at the end of the two-day mission, over thirty souls were prayed for and counselled as they accepted Jesus as Saviour and Lord. The following day, Jimmy went to collect all the posters and bring them back to his house. Nora had made something to eat, as per usual, and when Jimmy returned, he was breathless and agitated. As Nora inquired what was wrong, he said that as he was removing the poster from the Five-Ways Roundabout in Newry, he heard this voice declaring, "The train is coming, the train is coming."

FULL GOSPEL IN PORLAOISE

Putting all that behind us, we were invited down to Portlaoise some months later to a Full Gospel Businessmen's Fellowship, where I was the speaker. After I gave my testimony, people came forward for prayer. One young gypsy girl told me she was a Christian but weak in her faith. She wanted to share her faith with her family but lacked the strength to do so. I told her that the Scriptures speak from Acts chapter one, verse eight, about receiving power after the Holy Spirit comes upon you. "That's it," she said, "I need power."

As I prayed with her, the power of God hit her, and she fell backwards onto the floor ("slain in the Spirit"). As I looked down at her, I noticed that there was something demonic troubling her. Kneeling beside her, I commanded a spirit to leave her in Jesus' name. She immediately began to speak in tongues. As I helped her up, she asked, "What was I saying when I was on the floor?" "You were speaking in tongues," I said. She inquired what that was, and I said, "Come. I will show you from the Bible." "You can't," she said. "I can," I said. "You can't," she said, "For I cannot read or write." Here was this precious young woman, who had never heard of the Baptism of the Holy Ghost or of speaking in tongues, now not only having the gift but operating in it. I noticed that there were two ladies and a gentleman standing over by the door. They were shouting what Jimmy was shouting some months earlier: "The train is coming, the train is coming, the train is coming." I later learned that these people were from Alaska and were in Ireland on holiday. I never did find out what it all meant, but I believe that one day I will.

ANNAGHANOON

Over the years, I had been invited to speak at meetings at Annaghanoon Christian Ministries. This had been an old Elim Church built around 1926, which a small group of people had purchased in the early nineties during the times of the "Troubles" in Northern Ireland. It had been bought to be a place of healing for those troubled by the various situations happening in Northern Ireland at the time and was also a place where people could go to be ministered to for deliverance.

A man called Jimmy Winning was the manager of the place, and the trustees were from different churches and different denominations. Jimmy had a God-given gift for praying for people and setting people free from demonic forces and influences. By the time we had moved in with Esther in 2012, Jimmy had passed away. The place was now run by Robin Blakely. Robin would invite me to speak at his meetings whenever possible. One evening, when the meeting was over, Robin said he would love us to be involved with him in the ministry. We told him that we were open to his suggestion.

A year previously, a lovely lady called Jean Somerville, had spoken to us about getting involved at Annaghanoon, as it was affectionately called. It was like a God-given request. Her husband, Tom, had played a major part in setting up the ministry but he had also passed away. We recalled that after Jean had made that suggestion, we had gone to the car where we prayed and spoke to the Lord to say we would never push ourselves to make it happen, but we are willing to serve the Lord. Within days of Robin's suggestion, the trustees wanted to meet us. There was Rev Jim Hagan, Rev David Somerville and Peter Parkinson (a local businessman). They wanted to interview us, which seemed a sensible thing to do.

Later, they told us that they had a plan and believed that God was in the plan. They had prayed for someone to take over the running of the ministry, as Robin was getting older, and so were the majority of the trustees. They asked us what we thought of the idea, and believing we would be working under their authority, but possibly managing the Centre, we told them it was a good enough idea. We prayed about the plan and believed that God was in it. At a further meeting, as we sat there, they told us they had reconsidered the situation.

We had prayed to the Lord that if this was His plan, we were willing to be obedient, but if it wasn't then we wanted nothing to do with it. They told us how they had prayed and sought God for someone to continue the ministry rather than sell the property (there was an offer on the table for the purchase of the land and property). They then said that they were not able to give it over to us but had to sell it, as it was a charity. We were still not clear as to their intentions, and then Jim Hagan stood up and said, "We all believe that you are the right people to take over this place, and so we want to sell it to you. The requested price for the Centre, a two-bedroom flat, and enough parking area to park thirty cars was one pound sterling! The Centre could hold about sixty people comfortably.

As Shirley and I looked at each other in disbelief, we could do nothing but believe that this was God. So we now had our own place in Northern Ireland. They asked us what we would do with Robin, who had done a wonderful work here at Annaghanoon and had helped many people throughout the years. They were concerned that they may hurt his feelings, and we replied that Robin would be a consultant, but sadly, Robin passed away some weeks later, giving us a blank canvas for fresh ideas.

It was not long after we opened our doors that a young neighbour took very ill, and there was very little hope she would survive. Jim and Gladys, who are our neighbours and friends, came to ask if they could use the hall, as some people wanted to come together to pray into the situation. We met for prayer for the first week, and there were various reports of hope and healing, and every night, Monday to Friday we prayed, continuing the next week, bringing more concerns before the Lord. There were tears shed, and weeping could be heard at many of these meetings as we sought God for souls to be saved, people to be healed and other situations were prayed into. The wee neighbour was now out of hospital and doing well, but there were other situations that needed our prayers.

For four years, we held prayer meetings five nights a week until Covid 19 came, and we were obliged to stop for a season. During the day, Shirley and I would have people come in for prayer. For some, it was deliverance, and by now, we were confident in our calling and our place with God. We started a meeting every Friday evening and had people come to lead worship and others to preach or share testimony.

We have had some amazing meetings, and here, as in Benbecula many years previously, we have sensed the beautiful fragrance of the Lord in our midst. We have also known of angelic voices adding to our worship, but although many would frown on supernatural signs and wonders, we are convinced that such phenomena are simply proof that God is in our midst.

HIGHWAYS BYWAYS CENTRE

Since coming to Annaghanoon, we were obliged to change the name of the Centre, and it is now called Highways-Byways-Centre. Highways-Byways-Missions was the name of Shirley and my mission in Eastern Europe. We look back at the times we were here learning from Jimmy Winning, sleeping in what was then a damp wee room with wallpaper that would give you nightmares! We didn't know that one day, we would be sitting in his chair and sleeping in the same room we had slept in so many years previously. But now the flat was cleaned out, painted and made into a haven for us and many other people who were in need of a wee break from the struggles of life.

As you can understand, we cannot divulge any of the names of the people we have ministered to at this place, as it is in general very personal and private. Can I simply say that over our years here, we have helped many people and set many people free in Jesus' name.

I have permission to tell the story of Nichola, who came here for prayer. We knew her father and mother and had met her at another church where I was preaching. Nichola had a neurological disorder that caused her to be unable to walk properly, and it also affected her arms. There was an unsteadiness in her walk, and she should have been in a wheelchair, but her determined will and desire to be healed would not allow her to settle for what appeared to be the easy option.

Nichola was a beautiful lady who was a qualified nurse but had not worked for several years because of this disability. She had faith, determination and plans for what she would do when healed. She came here several times and had become our friend. One Saturday, with Shirley and another woman, she went shopping. Although wheelchairs were available in the shopping centres, Nichola refused to entertain the thought. They returned here to Highways-Byways-Centre early in the evening, and it began to snow quite heavily. Nichola had a mobility car and planned to head home, which was an hour's drive away. I asked her to consider staying with us, but she told me that there were situations she needed to attend to. Eventually, I persuaded her to stay with us until morning, when daylight would make her journey easier.

After some supper, Shirley went to help Nichola get ready for bed. It was decided that Shirley would take off the top and help her put on pyjamas. Nichola would do the bottom bit to preserve her dignity. As Nichola tried to raise her arms to assist Shirley to remove her top, there was an unnatural strength in her arms and they stopped to pray, believing that Jesus was near. As this increased strength seemed to invade her arms, they prayed, "Lord, if you can do this, you can heal Nichola's legs."

As Nichola stood up, the supernatural power was enabling her legs to be strengthened and she was marching on the spot. Joy and jubilation flooded their souls. We have a short corridor from the bedroom to the living room, and I was sitting on the settee in the living room when Nichola burst in, walking, dancing, skipping and running, but marvellously healed. We phoned our neighbours, Jim and Gladys, to come and witness this miracle. It was so difficult for us to believe, and we were looking for other people to confirm to us that we were not dreaming. We phoned another friend called Kathy, to come. Going to sleep that night was not easy because of all the excitement. Nichola had, without doubt, been touched by the hand of an almighty God and has made a remarkable recovery. We continue to thank God for His amazing love and power.

"DEAD" MAN RECOVERS

Some of the stories that happened can be very funny. I was asked to go and pray for an elderly statesman one day. I had previously met him and his wife, and reports were saying that he was very poorly. As I knocked on the door, I was welcomed by his wife, who ushered me into the bedroom where her husband lay in a hospital bed with the rails at the side. He was very weak and barely able to speak. I told him that I was there to pray for him, and his wife left the room, leaving me on my own with her husband. I tried to make mention of the Lord and our hope in Christ and bring him comfort, as I did not expect that he would have long to live.

It was now time to pray, and as I prayed, I kept my eyes open, whereas normally I would have them shut. Not long into my prayer, this lovely man's head fell backwards, his mouth opened, and he was motionless. I checked for breath, but there seemed to be none. There was no movement, and I thought that he had died. Moving close to his ear, I tried to talk to him, but there was no response. This would not be good for my CV. I pray for people, and they die!

I then had the predicament of how to break the news to his wife. "He's dead, Mrs.," seems hard and cold. "Oh, I am sorry Mrs., but your husband has stopped breathing and moving," did not sound right either. In the end, I thought I would make my way out and say nothing, as my medical qualifications did not allow me to make a judgment of whether he was dead or alive. She would find him a short time later when I was no longer around. That was the choice I made, leaving the "dead" man waiting for his wife to find him "dead."

This was not a brave decision, but that is what I did. I felt really bad that I did not have the gumption to do the right thing, and told Shirley. Shirley wanted me to do the right thing and go back, but I thought that it was too late. On his death certificate, it would say: "Died of boredom, listening to Donald Buchanan praying!"

That evening at the prayer meeting, a couple came in, "We heard that you were down praying for Mr. K today," they said. I was ready to deny it! But they continued: "He was so well when we called he was sitting up in bed, and his wife told us you had been round to pray for him!" I shouted Hallelujah, Hallelujah, Hallelujah! *"But God…"*

THE DEAD ARE RAISED

There have been a couple of situations where we do believe that people who had died came back to life. The first was back in Benbecula. One of our neighbours was a man who would have had problems with alcohol, and when he came off the booze, he would have convulsions and blackouts. One evening, his young daughter rushed into our house shouting, "It's Daddy! Something is wrong with Daddy!" With another man who had been visiting us, we rushed to the house. On arrival, we found the man spread over the chair. His face was black, and blood was coming from his mouth. He was motionless and lifeless.

Opening his mouth to see if he had swallowed his tongue, we were in panic mode, and finally, we cried out, "In the name of Jesus, we command the spirit of death to release this body and set this man free." We prayed again, demanding the spirit of death to be gone in Jesus' name. Suddenly, there was a movement and a cough. The man began to cough and splutter as his wife and children gathered around, crying in relief that God had given them back their husband and father. In all honesty, I believe that this man was released from the grip of death.

Another situation happened at our Centre many years later. Our preacher that evening was a gentleman whom God had used in healing and deliverance ministry. He was, without a doubt, a man of great faith. He had explained faith and the need to have faith, quoting various portions of Scripture as he did so. He had been speaking for some forty-five minutes, and then he collapsed. I was sitting at the back and heard Shirley's voice call through the crowd, shouting my name. Thinking that an audio loudspeaker had fallen off the wall and hit the preacher, I rushed to the front to find this man being worked on by a cardiac nurse called Gillian Clark from the Cookstown area (name used with permission), who was in the congregation. We actually had three nurses in the congregation that evening. People were shouting to send for an ambulance and send for a doctor, and the room was in chaos. I was told that when there is a situation, to appoint one person to be in charge and take all commands and orders from that person. Gillian was in charge. Gillian, who was actively involved, said there was no pulse and no breath as I stood astride this man lying on the floor.

I shouted a similar shout as I had done many years previously, "In the name of Jesus Christ of Nazareth, I command the spirit of death to leave this body now." It was with supernatural authority. For some unknown reason, I had supernatural faith to believe that all was going to be well. At that command, the body was aroused, and the preacher opened his eyes. Gillian, the nurse whom I had put in charge of the situation told us later that he was clinically dead. Taking my instructions from the lady in charge, we sent for a paramedic to check this man out. The paramedic came and checked out the preacher man and declared him fit and well to go home that evening but to visit his doctor at the earliest possible occasion. It could have been a disastrous situation, *"But God."*

On several occasions, we have seen instant healings. Amanda came from Kilkeel one night in absolute pain, suffering from sciatica. If you have ever suffered from sciatica, it not only controls your waking moments but also affects your sleep pattern. Amanda came forward, and the presence and power of God was there to heal. Instantly, the pain and discomfort left, and recently, Amanda confirmed that the pain has never come back.

Another local man came in for prayer one night. He had been a police dog handler. He was now a retired gentleman but was unable to raise his arms above his waist and wanted to do things around the house. One of the things he wanted to do was to mow the lawn. He was a believer and had been treated by the Health Service for some time, but to no avail. After talking to him and praying for him, we noticed that faith was bringing a release to this man's situation, and before he left the building, he was waving his arms above his head, totally healed.

Another young lady came one day in total fear of being near death, as her arm had swollen and was sore after having given a blood sample at the local doctors. Her arm was sore from her shoulder to her fingertips, and she was experiencing pins and needles in her hand and fingers. In the quietness of a moment, Shirley laid her hand on her arm and, simply, as the Scriptures say, that was all she did. There was no praying, praising, or any other action but to lay hands on the sick, and they shall recover. Within minutes, the pain was gone, the discomfort was over, the fear was lifted, and this young lady was calm and collected. It was a "suddenly moment" in the wonders of God.

Another family came here from Bangor. A lady had problems with her walking, and like Nichola, we were told it was neurological. After some encouraging faith-building conversation, we prayed for her, and she walked out our door, fully restored.

In the middle of all the wonders of God, we get to laugh at situations. Tina came here to our prayer meeting, and as the meeting ended, she asked for prayer. I stood beside her, and as we prayed, the power of the Spirit of God came over her, and she was going down backwards. She was wearing a loose crocheted cardigan, and her cardigan got entangled with a button on my jacket. Therefore, as she went down, I had to go down with her! As she lay there, under the anointing of the Spirit, I tried to disentangle my button from her cardigan, and my face was just over her face. If you have ever been "slain in the Spirit," you may be fully aware of everything around you, but you are so relaxed and in a state of total well-being that you are in no hurry to open your eyes or get up. Tina was totally relaxed in the Lord's presence.

As she opened her eyes, her first sight was my face. "What are you doing there?" she said. "I thought that it was Jesus breathing on my face." You can understand her disappointment!

HAPPY FEET

We travel on the Stena-line ferry from Ireland many times throughout the year. It is a journey of over two hours, and I use that time wisely by sleeping, as usually we have driven several hours to get to the ferry. We usually go to the cinema area, as the seats are more suitable for sleeping.

On this certain journey, I simply could not sleep. That day, a daft wee cartoon was showing, and as I tried to sleep, I heard the noise from the cartoon in the background. Eventually, I sat up and watched what I thought was a stupid little cartoon about a happy, wee penguin who danced. The name of the film was "Happy Feet," and I watched it until the end and thought no more about it. The following day, Shirley had an appointment with the dentist in Dungannon. I took her there, and as I waited outside, I noticed that the name of the business nearby was Happy Feet. It was a Podiatrist/Chiropodist clinic, and I did think it was a coincidence after watching Happy Feet the previous day.

Some days later, I bought a pair of shoes, and inside the box was a sheet of soft tissue paper with Happy Feet written on it. This was now more than a simple coincidence. One evening, some weeks later, I was preaching, and at the end of the meeting, people came for prayer. As I prayed for a man called Jackie, my feet began to dance (honestly!) They began to tap on the floor. I asked Jackie if he had a problem with his feet, to which he replied that often, after a hard day's work, his feet would be sore (as he worked as a mechanic and walked on concrete all day). As I prayed for him, my feet danced, and Jackie does not recall having sore feet since.

Now and again during times of worship or when I pray for people, I can sense a feeling in my feet to dance. It is one of those strange phenomena that I cannot explain, but I believe I have happy feet and that it is a God thing.

YOUNG MAN SET FREE

A lthough I do not want to divulge too many stories of people we have prayed for and prayed with over the years, I feel that Christians should be made aware of the people perishing for lack of knowledge of God's Word and understanding the wiles of the devil. I ponder and wonder if our Christianity has been demoted to a courteous call to a church once or even a few times every week, and that is the total sum of our worship and devotion to Christ the Lord.

Recently, as I prayed, I was reminded that the Christian believer is on a battlefield, not a playing field. The devil was, and is, out to kill, steal and destroy (John 10:10). A lovely young man came to see us one day. He had his own business. He was struggling with "voices in his head" telling him to kill himself. This would normally be seen as a mental health issue. The young man would be given medical advice and some tablets to help him cope with the situation.

I am in support of the Health Service, but I am also very aware that there are spiritual situations that need addressing spiritually. The young man told us that this problem never bothered him until he became a Christian. After he had surrendered his life to Jesus a few years earlier, he had been tormented by thoughts and suggestions of suicide and self-harm. He had been strong enough mentally to pray through the attacks but wanted to be free of this problem.

We inquired about his hobbies and the books he read. We asked if there was ever any involvement with occultist practices. We asked about the films he watched and the music he liked, to be told that he had at one time been caught up in what is known as heavy metal music. He told us that he listened to it at a volume that made the floor shake, and even his bed would vibrate as a result of the noise blasting from the speakers in his room. Quickened by the Holy Spirit, we sensed that this was the root cause of the problem, and we asked the young man to stand up as we prepared to pray for him. We were pleading and covering ourselves, our minds, and our belongings with the Blood of Jesus.

The young man renounced his involvement in this devilish music, and as we prayed, there was the manifestation of an evil spirit leaving him. His tongue came out of his mouth to a length physically impossible, and with a few groans and shouts, he was completely set free. Sadly, there will be many young men and women tormented by the devil who do not have access to spiritual help because the church in general has stopped believing in ministries which were commonplace in the life of Jesus and in the early church.

THE END IS NEAR

Whether it is a season, a life, or a book, they will all come to an end. The main reason I wrote this book was to encourage people to seek God with all their hearts, and the Scriptures say that they that fear the Lord shall do exploits. I look back on my life and simply say I have been blessed. I have had challenges, as many do, but with Jesus we shall overcome. There are many stories I could tell, but to maintain the privacy of some of the people we have helped over the years, I have not recorded them in this book.

Some of the stories in this book will be hard to believe for some people, and maybe the reason for that is that their knowledge of the Scriptures is limited in knowing and understanding the reality of the power of God. The Bible clearly says that, "Except a man be born again, he cannot see the kingdom of God." That verse of Scripture is as relevant today as it was the day it was spoken and subsequently written. It is found in John chapter 3 and verse 3. In the days when Jesus was ministering on the earth, His biggest enemies were the religious people. Today, many people are hoping that their religion, association or affiliation to a certain religion or religious body, will help them get to Heaven. The Bible states that Jesus said, "I am the way, the truth, and the life: no man comes to the Father, but by Me." That is found in John chapter 14 and verse 6.

Should you be burdened by your sin and your lack of concern about where you will spend eternity, then I can point you to the only Man who can save you, and that Man is Jesus Christ the Lord. In the Book of Acts chapter 4 and verse 12, it is written: "Neither is there salvation in any other: for there is no other name under Heaven given among men, whereby we must be saved." The word "saved" simply means that you will be saved from the punishment for sin, and that punishment is Hell. Being saved is being saved from Hell and having a place in Heaven reserved for you. God has not rejected you, but you may be rejecting God, and His way of salvation.

When I got saved in early December of 1983, I prayed a prayer something like this: *"Dear Lord Jesus, I am a sinner, and I believe that You came to earth to lay down Your life and die for sinners. I believe that in this transaction, You died for me, and I ask you to forgive me my sin, and I repent of my sin, and ask You to cleanse me from my sin and all of sin's effects. I ask You to come into my life, and be my Saviour and my Lord."*

The above prayer is simply an example of a salvation prayer. But I believe with all my heart that should someone pray it with repentance and sincerity, that Jesus will hear their prayer and answer their request. The Christian faith is not by works but by grace through faith. The faith that we speak of is in the finished work of Jesus Christ. He died for sinners, and if you are a sinner, He must have died for you. He paid the penalty a Holy God required to meet the demands of the Holy law which God had written for the good of all mankind.

At the end of this book, I want to ask myself the question: what would I say on my death bed if you were to come and visit me at that specific moment? I would tell you to make sure you are "born again." Make sure that you have not depended on some religious system or structure to make yourself right with God. Make sure that you have put your faith and trust solely and completely in the Lord Jesus Christ and Him alone.

Amen.

BV - #0041 - 110324 - C8 - 229/152/12 - PB - 9781739201821 - Gloss Lamination